The Monk CEO

OrangeBooks Publication

Smriti Nagar, Bhilai, Chhattisgarh - 490020

Website: **www.orangebooks.in**

First Edition, 2021

ISBN: 978-93-90489-60-2

Price: Rs.499.00

The opinions/ contents expressed in this book are solely of the author and do not represent the opinions/ standings/ thoughts of OrangeBooks.

Printed in India

ARJUNA IN BUSINESS

THE MONK CEO

Shree Guru

OrangeBooks Publication
www.orangebooks.in

Hariom

movement

Involuntary Transformation

www.hariom.life

Introduction

All CEOs and their incorporations in the world technically play a vital role, in the evolution of human consciousness and its management work of Nature.

There is an unseen management work that happens all time in the seabed, holistic and integrated consciousness of the whole cosmos. It is just like the work you do as CEO. Your CEO management work cannot be seen physically, but it appears in the employees' actions of your company. Your work can only be seen and understood by some, who have better minds. In the same way, the management work of the supreme consciousness cannot be known by normal minds, but it needs an inner eye to perceive. There is also a CEO for that cosmic consciousness management work and that incorporation is "Cosmic Incorporation of this whole creation" that sustains well for millions of years. Its CEO is not a body that you can perceive. It is "the supreme consciousness with supernatural management skills and unlimited cosmic energies. In the consciousness realm of every being, he silently works. Human consciousness and its evolution plays vital role in the evolution of cosmos.

CEOs and Businesses play a very important role in the human evolution, as they offer a platform to people on which they actually burn their karmas, which they owe to the cosmic womb of Nature. So, The Cosmic CEO and the Nature, work with businesses and CEOs in the consciousness realm which cannot be perceived by the naked eye.

This book is not just a book that contains mechanical message carrying some text, but its every text carries certain cosmic energies that will silently work with your subtle system in the background to energize it, so your process of gaining that inner eye gets initiated. With such inner eye, you can perceive water in milk and milk in water in your personal and business lives!

You will carry the energies that actually help your mind to see every sand crystal clearly, by separating it from its heap, not manually or mechanically but by mind!

This book is written being in union with the cosmic consciousness and thus it carries the message of it, in every word. As you read this book, you will feel that radiation within by its energy transmission.

In terms of human consciousness and its evolution, CEOs, politicians, federal administrators, professors, teachers, Spiritual Gurus and few others play a major role in the front-end of the world, which they are not aware. They actually carry huge unlimited cosmic energies behind them to do their jobs in harmony with the "Laws Of Nature" or the laws of "Cosmic Creation".

But how many of them really carry those unlimited cosmic energies is the question. From the cosmic management perspectives, they are actually given such importance, as they perform the "cosmic work" indirectly in their duties.

A CEO actually performs cosmic work in his duties, which he is not aware. There are so many people in the world, but why you alone are chosen to be the CEO? There is an unseen support, encouragement and energy given by the cosmic management system in the process of you being chosen as the CEO of your incorporation. From the cosmic sense, you are given that job of playing an unseen cosmic role that actually evolves the human conciseness. Do you know this? that you as the CEO, are playing a cosmic role from your deep within? If you know, then you are ready to become Arjuna, the chosen one by the Cosmic Driver, the CEO of the cosmos.

Who is Arjuna? You might be able to know a little background of him on the internet!

So you as the CEO, don't you think, you actually have that huge cosmic energy with you and the support of the whole cosmic governance system? You have it, in reality, but the point is how well, that cosmic energy is working with you and supporting you in the background? If you have its support, then you technically do some extraordinary work by your consciousness that always works round the clock across your business, in the background.

The Monk CEO is such book that helps you aware of your gigantic originality by which you will be able to feel the support of the unlimited cosmic energies. You, the CEO are actually limited by body in doing some fast and extraordinary actions in your business. But those extraordinary actions can be done with the help of the cosmic energies and its supreme CEO. Religions call that cosmic CEO as God! But from the cosmic creation and its management perspectives, he is the cosmic boss, the cosmic CEO or the Cosmic Driver. You can make the Nature and your consciousness work for you all times in the background, to do some phenomenal things that actually help not only you, your incorporation but the whole humanity and the world. Just by thoughts and mind, without any physical actions, several things can be achieved and executed in the world involuntarily, when you empower your consciousness.

These are some soul related works that happen in the deep integrated consciousness realm with the help of Nature. Every human actually thinks and takes actions by body out of that integrated consciousness, which is the source code of the whole cosmos!

The objects in the whole cosmos including all planets, living beings, your business, your employees, your customers, your family members, lifeless things and non-living beings are actually floating on the ocean of integrated consciousness of theirs, which cannot be seen. That is actually their true self. When someone works from that true-self they do extraordinary works in their lives and in their businesses.

This book will lead you to the technologies and methods of taking help of the cosmic CEO and unlimited energies of Nature, to do your job well and acquire prosperity. Every CEO already has this opportunity given by the cosmic management system as they not only work for their incorporation, but indirectly they play a more vital role in the cosmic evolution. But many of them are not aware of it and they do not know the methods of taking the help of those unlimited energies. The cosmic boss and Nature are ready to give the CEOs, unlimited energies, which they can use in transforming their businesses and lives, provided, they are ready to become like Arjuna!

Monk CEO means, a Yogi in Jeans, A Yogi in the business suit and a Warrior Yogi who works with the gigantic energies of Nature for the true prosperity of the holistic self in which, business, personal life, employees and everything is included! Arjuna was a warrior Yogi who worked with the cosmic CEO to do an unforgettable and phenomenal work of bringing balance in the human consciousness. His Yoginess is not seen outside but carried inside and perceived by only few who have inner eye. But his warriorship is seen externally by ordinary people. Yogi is misunderstood by the world that, he is a monk and sits by closing eyes, doing nothing! But he works by consciousness which has major impact in the worldly matters and his work is not seen outside. There is another type of Yogi who participates in all actions of life actively but by carrying that Yoginess inside. Nature needs such Yogis more in the world today, as they can transmit their energies being in the middle of chaotic world and that yogi is Karma Yogi. A CEO has such opportunity given by the Nature and if the monkhood is carried inside in an unseen way with his business outfit, there he becomes Arjuna!

This book will reveal several cosmic management perspectives that will help you understand your true existence and its purpose in this whole cosmic atmosphere. This book will also introduce you to preliminary methods by which you will be able take the help of Cosmic CEO and the unlimited energies of the Nature.

This whole atmosphere of the world is a cosmic womb in which its governance works silently in the background of every business and being. Just like the way you know very well about your industry, in your business, you are required to know this atmosphere and the holistic industry of cosmic womb and its operational mechanisms. If you know cosmic womb and its operations, you can function well in your business and life to prosper easily instead of draining out your energies by going against its actual directions. By knowing cosmic womb and its actual atmosphere, you will be able to take its help, evolve faster and prosper easily and involuntarily in your life and business.

This book carries cosmic energies that will help you transform along with its knowledge related to cosmic governance. The process of your transformation gets initiated, as you read this book, because it will transmit those cosmic energies to you. This book will also reveal couple of initial methods by which you can tune to the frequency of cosmic CEO and Nature to take their energies, help and guidance to prosper your personal life and your business INOLUNTARILY.

INVOLUNTARY TRANSORMATION of human consciousness is the next level technology of the cosmic CEO and Nature and this book is written as part of its work, with its energies that radiate.

Transformation in life takes high amount of individual efforts and it's a very long journey. It is also a very slow process and it does not happen fast with individual efforts. Imagine you, holding the hand of your child and guiding her in every step of writing her exam. You work through her and finish the exam fast, while she earns the excellent results and you earn the happiness! Your work through her gets her involuntary success and the happiness you get in that process, merges you, in your true universal consciousness!

Nature tried to evolve the human consciousness in several other means so far on the earth but humans have lost their energies to transform on their own, which is the reason why this "involuntary transformation technology" is brought down to transform you involuntarily, like the way you helped your child in the example given.

As part of its cosmic work, this book is the work of cosmic consciousness working through me. Just like the way, your child wrote the exam with your help, I have written this book with cosmic consciousness working through me and thus it is the divine effort of cosmic consciousness that emits its energies through every text of this book. So this book is not regular or common individual human effort. This book is a practical proof of COSMIC INVOLUNTARY work of its consciousness, which anyone can experience by tuning to the cosmic CEO, and excel in their lives and duties while emitting the cosmic energies that transform and prosper their environment, families, businesses and society. Purposely, no editing efforts are made by any individual to maintain the original cosmic consciousness behind this book. It is intended that, some efforts are also made by the reader to KNOW its text, which will initiate the actual journey within, to listen to the "Cosmic CEO".

Even if few CEOs become Arjunas and work with the guidance of the cosmic CEO, they would perfectly do the justification to their role and life for which THE NATURE, the COSMIC WOMB would always be thankful to them and reap its

UNLIMITED BENEFITS and PROSPERITY to them and their businesses.

My loves to you, your businesses and families

- Hariom, Shree Guru

Special Thanks

My special thanks and loves to Arjunas in Business, Shree Raghava Akshintala (COO) and Shree Vikram Dintyala (CEO) of Savitr Software, Hyderabad, India.

My special thanks and loves to Malin Govinder and Jessie Govinder who work like Arjuna in their business. They are living with their son, Josua in Johannesburg, South Africa.

My loves to Shiv Sudheer and Sindhu, from Trivendram, India who are Arjunas in their business.

My loves and special thanks to Shree Maha Avatar Babaji, who is always around in the support of Hariom Movement. He is like the Sun who keeps shining for the welfare of the humanity.

My special thanks to my wife, Shree and my daughter Veda, who support me in doing my involuntary cosmic job.

Index

Chapter-1

You Are A Creator.. 1

Chapter-2

The Monk CEO His Unlimited
potentials, wealth, Prosperity and Energy 16

Chapter-3

Arjuna And Krishna The right
combination 30

Chapter-4

The Purpose of Creation 35

Chapter-5

Creation And Strategy 57

Chapter-6

Cosmic Management Team 74

Chapter-7

Position of Your Business In Cosmos 86

Chapter-8

The Nature 94

Chapter-9

The Field of Womb... 107

Chapter-10

Time And Space And Its Evolution........................ 120

Chapter-11
CEO And Karma.. 132

Chapter-12
CEO And Simplicity.. 141

Chapter-13
Maya or Illusion.. 148

Chapter-14
CEO Being The Hero, Arjuna 152

Chapter-15
The Driver.. 172

Chapter-16
Tuning To The Preceptor...................................... 180

Chapter-17
Karma Vs Universal Karma.................................. 205

Chapter-18
Dharma 211

Chapter-19
Change In Cosmic Management........................... 218

Chapter-20
Making The Nature Work For You 227

Chapter-1

You Are A Creator

This chapter is more like a conversation between you and me. It is a subtle conversation that will logically lead you to the truth of your own true self. The conversation could easily slip out of the mind and hence, try to be more alert.

Business means, you do something for the welfare of others in the world and by giving that service, you sustain with good comforts in the process. Business in the real sense is "doing something for the welfare of others or the world".

Business also means, you as the creator or the owner or the CEO of the business, you expanded your consciousness from a point of thought. Primarily, the thought which was like a "point of birth" from where the whole thought got expanded and then many other chains of thoughts were processed, strategized and then it became a vision. So it is all expansion. What kind of expansion it is? It is an expansion of your consciousness that started from a single point and then it got expanded further and became a vision. Then it just did not stop there, it started taking, material presence of it, in the physical world by which you took some space, you bought some office related infrastructural things and then hired some people. Let us say you name your company “X Incorporation”

You need to be so attentive in following this analogy that is going to be presented. The analogy will slip so quickly out of your mind which gets you out of the enjoyment of it. You will enjoy because, you are going to meet your true-self by reading it.

Now the question is – “who is this X incorporation actually?”. Is it a thing? A body? Let us say, someone comes and asks you “show me your X incorporation”. Then you take him to your physical office and show him. Probably you also show him the federal incorporation certificates recognized and given by the Government. Is it by truth “X Incorporation”?

Who is “X Incorporation” actually? The answer is YOU. You are the X incorporation. Who are you? is it your body that produced originated the primary thought from where all this STORY of X incorporation began? No right? Can you show your body to that man and say, this is X incorporation?

The truth is, it is your consciousness that produced the “primary thought” of doing something. In your consciousness the birth of X incorporation took place. Then that primary thought got expanded further in your mind and then it took the physical form in the physical world. Even if your X incorporation is existing in the real world, it is actually existing, in your consciousness first. Every day your business is expanding in your physical world and it is also expanding in the realm of your consciousness. The truth is that the expansion takes place first in the consciousness and then, it happens in the real world.

So, technically your consciousness is spread across the physical "X Incorporation". By mind and by consciousness, YOU are actually that "X Incorporation". But not your body. So who are you now? You are that mind and consciousness but not body!

So you and your X Incorporation to which you gave birth are not separate by mind and consciousness. You and the incorporation are one and the same. Your consciousness is the source of the birth of "X Incorporation". After incorporating, the company, the work does not end there. It keeps expanding further both in terms of its services to the world and its physical presence.

That means, it is, expansion of your consciousness. That also means that it is the expansion of your consciousness, technically.

What does this expansion of consciousness get you, to the creator of this company? Ultimately, the bottom line of the answer is happiness. It is giving immense of happiness to you when you see many people working for the company, when you see the customers of your company praising your services and work and when you see the expansion of business to many states and countries and so on. You also feel happy, when your employees are happy. Who are your employees? What are your computers, tables, chairs and that entire infrastructure in your company? Whose instructions and directions are working in your employees? Directions, instructions, suggestions and all are yours right? The source of these directions, instructions and suggestions is energy. Whose energy it is? It is your energy that is working in your employees. You basically transmit your vision, advises and directions to your managers and they further transmit them to the down level employees. At this point, we should remember, the way, the coach of a football team, transmits his energies to all his team members. The coach puts his head to each player's head, deeply looks into the eyes of each player and transmits all his vision, directions and advises in the form of his energy. He inspires them, energizes them and encourages them. This is a very high end of spiritual technique followed by the football coaches.

It is actually the spiritual energy of the coach that energizes the players and in reality; it is the energy of the coach that works in the players. But ordinary people cannot see the energy of the coach working in the players.

In the same way, it is your energy that works in all employees of your company.

After reading this whole thing, physically you may accept but the energy aspect must be a surprise for you.

So your energy is in them that means who is there in them? The answer is, it is you, who is there in them. But who is that YOU? Is it your physical body which is there in them?

No, the answer is, your consciousness which is working in them and it carries your vision, your directions and advises along with your energies. That is the whole package of consciousness that works like magnetism in the field of your business and the magnet is you but you are not actually that physical magnet in reality you are that magnetism that is spread in and out of every employee and all things in your business. The employees as they are humans, they carry their own energies just like football players but your energy like a SUN works in them that makes them shine! It is actually your source of energy that is shining them, though they have their own limited energies.

So you might start a business in a small way but as your consciousness expands and as your business expands, you start becoming more like a father of the business from where you get to see all your employees and other stakeholders as your children or your own limbs. You might feel bad if anyone of them suffer in their lives. That's because your consciousness is spread everywhere across your incorporation. Not just in people alone. If you lost few computers in your company, you feel bad because your consciousness is also spread in those computers that you lost. So your consciousness is there in living beings of employees and also in non-living beings of things in your corporation. This is nothing but split of your consciousness into those people and things. Because of that, if you lose some computers or infrastructure, you will feel bad. You will also feel bad, if you lose some employees or if they have any problems and so on. Do not bring the non-energetic and mechanical modern thought of "you are emotional" into this context. We will discuss that on a separate note, later.

The point of this expansion of consciousness is discussed in a greater level is, to give you the example of consciousness and its expansion.

This creation also came into existence in the same way.

You must have started your business by giving one type of service or product to the people but later you must have expanded to, many types of products and services. It is also the expansion of your consciousness in creating new products and things in your corporation that first take place in your consciousness. In the same way, in this cosmic creation also various living beings and various worlds came into existence as the creation got evolved.

Another point of understanding is that, you established the corporation with the primary objective of "doing something for the welfare of others". The service or the company you thought of, technically came out of your love, which is the primary ingredient in your consciousness itself. Love is from where the creation starts and that's how the creation that comes out of you is much closer to your heart and emotions. You might have thought about a service and a product to sell in the market. But what does it do ultimately? It basically gives some comfort, some value addition to the lives of others, who buy your product or service. But the ORIGIN of the thought in a hidden way which you do not know is – "doing something for the welfare of others" which again drills down to the source of "love and its other sibling elements such as compassion, good intentions, helping others and doing good to others".

The question is why do you want to do good for others? – You feel like that because the others you think are not actually others! Physically they are like other objects without any physical connection. In the deep integrated consciousness, as it is one, you feel that connection with others naturally and that is the reason why you feel like doing good to others.

So, who are others actually?

The others you think are not actually others, but your-own-others.

They are many people in the world. But the entire world will use your service and product? No. Only few people who need your service and product will buy from you. So from where those customers are born (from the perspectives of your incorporation)?

They are born out of your product creation itself. Before the physical creation of your product or service, before the inception of your company, the customer segment was also planned and strategized in your consciousness.

So in your consciousness, you already gave birth to your customers. So customers are also born out of your consciousness itself.

To put it in another way, what made the customers buy your product and service? A customer is your partner actually. He is part of your consciousness. He is not separate from you. That is why, he is called partner, another limb of yours. They are your-own-others. The answer to all these questions is, the customers also produced out of your consciousness, from your business perspectives (not of the world). It is your consciousness out of which your products and services came along with customers.

So, in your consciousness both living beings and non-living beings are there and they also got evolved as your business got expanded which means as your consciousness got expanded.

So the others you think of i.e. about your employees, your infrastructural things, your customers, your products, services AND YOU are all one and the same. That practically proves that "there are no others". There is only YOURSELF by the truth. That yourself is your consciousness which is there everywhere, in all those who are associated with you.

You (meaning, your consciousness) are the creator of your world (which is your incorporation). Your world is your incorporation. Your consciousness is spread across the whole incorporation (which is your creation). You are there in everyone (people) and also in things (such as computers etc). Your consciousness which is spread in your world is your own small pool of consciousness.

Understand this point in a simple way, wherever your awareness goes, your consciousness follows in the background. Your consciousness is like a shadow that does not need anything; it just follows you, wherever your awareness goes. Your awareness always roams around the small world of your creation which is your business. It also goes around your family, other worldly matters and other personal matters which we can keep aside in this context, as you did not plan them in your consciousness at the time of incepting your business. They are away from the creation of your business.

So for the creator of this universe this whole universe is his world which is the biggest pool of consciousness. There is no other bigger pool of consciousness than his. He is actually that pool of consciousness itself. In that pool of consciousness, every other small pools of consciousness exist. That is the supreme pool or ocean of consciousness. That supreme ocean of consciousness silently supports all its contents in the background in terms of creation, sustenance and destruction works. That pool has a governance system, it has its own laws and it has its own CEO whom, religions call God but he is technically the supreme consciousness. It also has its own management system and it has its own responsibilities of sustaining all the small pools in it.

If you compare this whole analogy, just like your consciousness being there throughout your corporation, God's consciousness is there in all the living beings and non-living beings in the whole cosmos.

In your case, your own consciousness is split into to many particles (all people and things associated with your company) which created all your incorporation and it was formed out of your love of serving others in the world.

In the same way, with creation of the cosmos, the pure consciousness in order to feel its own self because it does not have a body, it's got split itself into many particles which further evolved materialistically. Your incorporation was also created to experience the self in others.

The truth you need to know is, though you are in a way creator of your own business, in the background, there is an unseen support of the biggest pool of consciousness in creating your dream. Its governance system, its responsibilities of sustaining the creation makes it to support in creation and sustenance of your dream of starting a business. There are several factors it takes into consideration such as your intentions, your hard work, your passion, your emotions, your karma, your love for starting the business and all.

The oceanic pool of consciousness actually is ready to play a bigger role in sustaining your business than in creation. Humanity has taken so far its help in more creation but not in sustenance. For the involvement of its cosmic energies, in sustaining your energies, it needs you, seeking its help being in harmony with its laws is essential. Just seeking its help would not help you at all. Being in harmony with its laws with the combination of seeking its help will make it majorly involve in sustaining your business.

That is the ultimate objective of this book. Creation is easy to certain extent but sustaining a business is a greater challenge.

Though you are a creator of your business technically from the physical world perspectives, your small pool of consciousness needs the help of oceanic pool of consciousness because your consciousness is a limited personality and it is not a universal personality. You carry the elements that limit your consciousness such as pride, prejudices, anger, greed, lust, misusing authority, individual ego and so on. These are all, the gate holders that do not let your consciousness expand whereas the creator of the cosmos is pure selfless consciousness that is universal and that does not carry any of those limitations. So it produces pure unlimited energy that can run its incorporation for millions and millions of years whereas your energy is limited and due to those weaknesses and attachments, your incorporation goes through several ups and downs, challenges and existential issues. Your incorporation only lasts at max, if it is great, to a century or so.

The creator or the CEO of the cosmos manages it abiding its laws of creation, though they are actually born out of his consciousness. Though he is the creator, when it comes to managing his creation, he follows his own-created laws very strictly. That is his strength actually. His energies keep increasing as he follows mainly those laws. He is actually those laws and those laws are him.

He also has huge cosmic team members who do not go out of its laws and that law is called THE DHARMA. How many ever challenges may come, the management operation of the cosmos never goes out of THE DHARMA.

It never compromises for its existence. His cosmic management job is always in harmony and he is always in yogic state to manage this whole cosmos. In the history of the creation, he faced dangerous situations that could wipe out the whole creation, but yet, all times, he could get out of those situations. The CEO of the cosmos owns the whole cosmos but yet he is detached from it and operates it in a detached way out of pure consciousness by not having any attachments like our worldly CEOs.

His family and business is this whole cosmos. He owns all but yet he disowns all. He is in the war zone of dangers, with attractive comforts, money and all but yet, he is detached from all of them. So I call him "The Monk CEO" of the cosmos. The worldly CEOs can adopt his style of managing the cosmos, in their businesses and thus they could also become Monk CEOs.

He is a yogi, monk, but yet, he has a huge family. He is a monk who does not own anything but yet the owner of the whole creation. He is in the middle of war zone, but yet in peace and harmony. Such CEO he is. He is hurt when you are hurt but yet, no tears will come from his smiley eyes.

Whereas, you as the CEO, in the process of facing several challenges you get disturbed and you go out of the DHARMA (which are laws of Nature) and operate your business which further produces more problems in future for your business, as per the laws of Nature.

You go out of the way for temporary fixes, because of the fear factor. So the business becomes a kind of situationally managed out all these disorders of limited personality. It is due to lack of the true cosmic perception and energy in you that gets you limited.

Some companies become so big at times like lions and they could even eat up the riders, the CEOs. Just like in car driving, in the driving process of the business, there will be never ending unexpected situations that come. How much ever you strategize, plan and use several business analytical softwares, there are always other factors that cannot be managed.

You are the CEO of your incorporation. The creator of the whole cosmos is also managing the whole show of creation by being the CEO. Technically, your business is playing a cosmic role and your business is supported by the Nature and its unlimited energy, which is the oceanic pool.

You as a CEO would need energies and you basically gain energies by getting motivated by others in the world right?

You basically get impressed and follow the footsteps of various other CEOs and successful people in the world by probably reading their books and so on. You might implement some of them in your business and in your life and experience their results, to certain extent. But they are all just limited in terms of consciousness and energies, with all those mentioned weaknesses. But whom should you actually imitate and get inspired by? Whom should you actually follow? You as a child obviously follow your father right? Not another brother of yours who is born along with you. You might wonder how you can follow him. There is a mechanism to invoke the Cosmic CEO to follow his directions and the wonder thing is, it does not cost you!

You can tune to the frequency of this CEO of the cosmos by which you can absorb his cosmic energies, his operational ways and unlimited management techniques to manage your business well.

Chapter-2

The Monk CEO

His Unlimited potentials, wealth, Prosperity and Energy

In the previous chapter you got logically known that you were consciousness and it is not just pure due to all disorders, traits and karma. Karma is the work that you owe to the world.

Unlike all people, the bodiless pure supreme consciousness is so pure and it is called supreme because, out of its purity, it has unlimited energy by which it manages the whole show of creation.

You can imagine him like a nucleus that is lost, in its own self which does not need nor aware of anything else. That is purely lost in its own self that generates the energy. It is like magnetism that is not aware of anything. It is just aware of its own self. Magnetism also has awareness because it will recognize the iron thing placed in its field. But magnetism is lost into its own self and it does not need anything externally except physical magnet, for its sustenance.

If you check some saints from India, they meditate and unite their small pools of consciousness into universal pool of consciousness, which is their true self. They remain like that for few days, months and years together.

When they open their eyes and get into activities in the world, they carry those cosmic energies. The works they do radiate in the world and have greater impact in the world. These saints also would have their own limitations and their meditation would only last for few days or years. But imagine, the forever existing bodiless nucleus lost in its own self (tapas) and imagine the kind of energies that nucleus generates. It is not just energy. It is consciousness coupled with energy. For your quick understanding, consciousness is like magnetism of a magnet. This way, you understand easily and feel it and it does not need much explanations.

The energy of the nucleus splits into three energies mainly. One energy creates the world; second energy sustains or manages the world and third energy that dissolves the world.

That second energy is in a specific way called "The Sustenance Energy or the Management Energy" is the one that actually runs the whole show of creation as a CEO. That specific energy has unlimited management capabilities, arts, skills and unlimited energies to deal with any situation in creation.

His main responsibility is to make sure that its laws i.e. "dharma" is followed in the world. Dharma means, laws of Nature. To run a corporation, it is must that everyone should follow its laws, rules and regulations. Without following its laws, rules and regulations, it does not matter how great ever one is and how great ever value addition one does. Such employee or partner will always be painful and he could do any wrong doing, one day with the firm.

Dharma means, Laws of Nature which is like the laws of your company. You have a law like everyone should show up in the office by 10 AM and everyone should follow it including you, the CEO of the company. It is just a small example to say. If you find that some employees are attending the office late, you cannot show your authority and ego by saying, “everyone should come on time and I am the CEO so I can come late”.

Without talking to anyone, you can discipline all just this way – You start coming to office on time. In few days, you will find that all employees naturally falling in harmony with the laws of the company. Even then, if someone does not show up on time, then it shows his arrogance and on him, you can take some action.

That kind of CEO is this CEO of the creation. For the laws of Nature, he can cut his own head in case, something goes wrong with him. For the management of the creation primarily DHARMA is very important. This is the reason why he always remains in the state of yoga. It is a state of perfect discipline and harmony out of which he does actions. After the Dharma, everything else follows in creation such as love, devotion and all.

There are several people who talk about lot of godly matters and spiritual matters but they hardly follow this thing called DHARMA. When one does not follow the DHARMA, then he does not carry any energies and he cannot transform himself or others. If you are a cigarette smoker and you being failed in controlling your small weakness, you cannot advise others on transformation matters.

Energies matter a lot to every soul, especially to the CEOs. Energies move people. Energies move things and work behind people to implement greater works.

The cosmic CEO, as part of his cosmic management strategy, to manage the world better, human society is classified into four segments. First segment is "the spiritual advisors" community. They basically spend all their time in meditation and selflessly live for the welfare of the world. They live a pious and disciplined life without ego, expectations, without lust, without anger, without even passion for anything, without desires and all. They spend their time purely in god-realization. They live a yogic life. Such community is important in the human society who can advise the political leaders, governments, administrators and the people. Because all these people work for the welfare of the society and their operations are very essential to sustain the society. Spiritual leaders of all religions mainly fall in this category. This community plays vital role in the society being untouched by illusion, money and all. But this community itself has become dark today. Those who are meant to help all others, they became spoiled and today, they do not receive any divine messages and they do not even practice spirituality well. They only show off their spirituality externally to attract people. They also need to be away from all pompous way of living and live closer to divinity by doing spiritual practices. But they do not have all those today. Their activities became a kind of business for them now. They use their spirituality to attract political leaders, business men, movie actors etc. to show their importance in the society and to attract more money for their businesses. Some of this community spoiled to a level of committing crimes. They are also playing roles in division of the society and communal fights.

The second community is of political leaders and federal administrators, who rule the people as per the laws of Nature. They take advises from the spiritual community said above and function their duties well. This community is heavily corrupted in the world. They totally misuse their authority and power to gain more money for their personal lives. They cheat all people in various ways and get that money. They also establish various businesses and to run those businesses well, they purposely get into politics to safeguard their mistakes. As political leaders they would have authority by which they can cover all their dark activities. This community is also spoiled to a level even to commit big crimes to sustain in their powers. This community majorly deals with bribery, money laundering, womanizing and many other things that are not acceptable publicly.

The third community is the Business Community. They also do their business as per the Dharma or laws of Nature and function in their lives. They help the whole society with required economics and they indirectly do their cosmic job, by giving people a platform to burn their karmas. This community has also fallen and gone into managing businesses against the laws of Nature. To protect their business and their positions, they do several actions against the laws of Nature. Business community is also dealing with bribery, money laundering, womanizing and many other things that are not acceptable publicly.

The fourth community is the doers community. They do various works and professions who work on their own and also work with governments and businesses. These are helpless people who don't have any direction in the society living for the sake of sustenance and in that process; they commit any kind of mistakes and crime.

The three main sections of the society do their cosmic duties indirectly so that the people down below them can live well in the world. But none of them function properly today in the world and hence they are not at all able to do their cosmic duties and thus, Nature has totally pulled out its energies to support them.

Incorporations also have the same structure in their operations like the above strategy of the creator. In your companies, you have advisory board, main management team, middle management team and others, who work in various departments.

The same strategy is followed by the Monk CEO, the creator to manage his incorporation of this world. The cosmic CEO, does not much involve in the governance of the Nature. It will run as long as it does not have any problems in it. But when the problems in its, governance system, it will seek the help of its CEO to involve. When he involves with his consciousness, then he will start repairing those problems.

Just like our governments mainly make sure that all people follow the STATUTORY rules of the country such as everybody should pay taxes, everyone should follow the law and live peacefully without causing any disturbances in the society, God's government also mainly focuses on its cosmic laws and dharma. God's government is called, Nature.

Our governments make sure that all their administrative departments run as per their laws and if the law is followed by all people of the country, then obviously the rate of crime and other illegal activities would be in their limits. The governments and various leaders also campaign about peace, happiness, love and all such things in public. They primarily they focus on THE DHARMA, the laws of government. If Dharma is there, rest all fall in place automatically. Primarily law and order in the countries need to function well which is nothing but Dharma.

Dharma or following the laws of the country does not apply to any specific set of people or religion or creed. They apply equally to all people and all religions the same. Following laws of government applies to all people living in the country right? In the same way, the Dharma of Nature applies to all religions and all people in the whole cosmos. It also applies to the Sun, to the Moon, to all planets, to all five elements and so on. They also need to function as per the cosmic laws and do their duties.

In the same way, for the creator CEO, Dharma becomes his predominant duty. That is the reason why, all religions in the world primarily teach discipline to the people. By following religions, people get disciplined and follow the laws of Nature well.

Sun, Moon, five elements and all who are part of the cosmic management team (employees of the cosmic incorporation) are also required to work as per the laws of Nature.

For this specific reason, religions came into existence and all religions teach devotion, love in the name of god and following certain disciplinary life. We modern men shy away from our religious practices, because we call ourselves modern which is actually making the ways for all of us to not to follow discipline in life. As modern men, we have our own ways to commit mistakes, we have earned attitude of covering our mistakes or doing mistakes in a mask and that mask name is modernization.

Modernization means, development right? We are modernizing all assets and things in our world but we don't really modernize ourselves. We are actually de-modernizing ourselves everyday by increasing our weaknesses, bad habits etc, which we call modernization. Mobile phones, softwares, all things that we use are upgrading everyday by modernization. But we are not upgrading ourselves, our downgrade ourselves day by day which we mask it saying "modernization".

Modernization should teach people to expand more, unite with all religions, but yet following their own religious practices well. Modernization does not mean, leaving your religious practices in which you are actually born. Religions also do not mean religious fanaticism that goes on creating hatred towards other religions. Unlike the today's world, in old days, people had less mobility and to manage themselves well with proper direction in life, various religions got born to show the ways to their people. But today, due to high mobility and globalization we all mix up which is good but at the same time, it does not mean, you leave your religions and it also does not mean that you go overboard by hating other religions. That balance is Yoga, the science of living in harmony. Yoga is a science of Nature in which all exist and it does not belong to any specific religion or any country in specific.

If yoga is the science of creation and along with religious practices if Yoga is practiced, transformation in all aspects of life will come. Yoga so far was practiced, but this book will introduce you to Involuntary Yoga that will transform you involuntarily so that you can experience the prosperity in life.

In terms of humanity, the cosmic CEO's responsibility is to make sure that the Dharma is followed well which is easily possible by controlling all the above said four communities in the human society. That means, he actually works with those four communities and their authorities. He not only works alone, his entire cosmic departments also work with all those authorities on the earth.

If the dharma is followed first, obviously prosperity, peace, love, humanity and all such things will flourish on the earth. Then, Nature the governance system can do its duty well.

Nature is like the governance system. Imagine you commit a crime and you do not cooperate with the police. Imagine, you say to the police that you are a great man with power and you cannot be arrested and so on. If it happens like that with you, tomorrow that can be repeated by various other people in the country. If everyone says the same thing, then obviously The Law is not able to do its job and law is out of its place.

So then, the law and order would be suffering in the country. Then the police men say to the government that they are helpless and the citizens are not cooperating. Then, all those police officers go helpless, except watching all the crime happening in the society. Then obviously some reformation needs to happen in the government. Probably new government has to come or federal administrators need to wake up and support the police and other forces to make sure that the law falls in place.

Every day we here lot of news and campaigns from the government authorities and administrative authorities about "the importance of following the law". Their campaigns also remind people about the punishments. Governments always run such campaigns to keep the law and order in control.

In the same way, the works of such campaigns continue always in the cosmic incorporation too, which is one of the responsibilities of the cosmic CEO.

As part of that process, The CEO of the creation always gets open to communicate with all the authorities of these four segments of the society of the world.

It is his job, to make sure of Dharma being followed in the world irrespective of the religions, creeds and sects.

The CEO of the creation has surplus amount of money, unlimited power, authority, unlimited energies, skills and arts to manage all the cosmos. Money, prosperity, power, various unlimited potentials always live with him so that he can face any kind of hard situations in the cosmos. The negative energies always create various danger situations in the cosmos that could harm the whole creation. It requires a great art of dealing with them and unlimited potentials and energies to come out of those dangerous situations.

So, because he is ready to be accessible by the authorities of the said communities, the CEOs of the businesses can tune to the frequency of the CEO of the creation and gain some potentials of the cosmic CEO so that they can manage their businesses pretty well.

As said above, if Dharma is followed, money, prosperity, power, unlimited energy, unlimited potentials and all will follow. All these powers are basically the spiritual energies of the cosmic CEO. Imagine these potentials, skills, purity of consciousness; good traits etc. of the cosmic CEO are like a software package and imagine that they all can be loaded into you, so you and your businesses can transform.

There is a way to tune to the cosmic CEO by your mind. Then your transformation will start automatically, as his software gradually loads into you. You can find yourself the transformation happening in few days, after starting such practices.

Do not think that the cosmic CEO will work by talking to you. No, his energies will slip into you with his CEO qualities and potentials which will work in you automatically.

You as CEO, need the same qualities and potentials in your personality, like the cosmic CEO. But can you learn all those qualities by reading books?

Can you quit smoking by reading just a book? If certain spiritual energies are loaded into you, you will be able to quit smoking easily without much individual efforts of yours.

Imagine the movie, Matrix, the first part. Remember, the hero NEO asking his programmer to load "loads of guns" in to him. He also asks to load a program of helicopter to fly it.

In the same way, when you tune to the frequency of the cosmic CEO, the software programs of his supreme soul energies will start automatically loading into you and you will start transforming involuntarily. The loading and transformation happens gradually but not all of a sudden!

When you start transforming, you will find automatically quitting many bad habits (not just external bad habits), bad habits such as hating others, not being able to control anger, jealousy, controlling others, dominating others, showing off your power and money to others, cheating others, tricking others, harming others, paying low to others and all these.

When such bad habits start going away from your system, in parallel, you will start attracting more money, more business, people and so on. It is a parallel activity like, on one hand, the disorders keep unloading and on the other hand cosmic CEO's energy keeps loading by making you attract more prosperity, money, more business and so on.

This book will present you more about the science of cosmic creation, its laws and about the importance of your existence and then after this education, you will be given the methods of "tuning to the frequency of the cosmic CEO".

Chapter-3

Arjuna And Krishna

The right combination

If you do not know anything about Krishna and Arjuna, you can probably check on internet to know the basic information. But, here you will find knowledge that you don't get on internet.

One thing that should be noted before going forward is – where Arjuna and Krishna are there together, there, you will find prosperity, victory, joy, authority, power, supreme peace and the support of Natural Forces.

It is a wrong opinion and belief in many people about spirituality that it is something that will make you weak or something that makes you leave your weapons and leave companies, family and go to Himalayas.

Arjuna also thought the same thing when he was there on the earth. But spirituality that was meant for him was to sharpen his skills more and act as per the laws of Nature by taking the help of all forces of Nature. That exceptional skill was added to his personality when Krishna entered into his life.

Krishna is the supreme consciousness, which is spread everywhere, in and out of every being. In that field of supreme consciousness everything and every being is there. Krishna is that super pool of consciousness or oceanic consciousness in which all are included. It's because of that field of super consciousness alone you are able to perceive all other objects in its field, which is this world. Do not call that field like space or void etc. No, it's like an unseen magnetic field existing without physical magnet. You cannot see its field, but you can know the existence of magnetic field by placing an iron element. In the same way, you cannot see this supreme consciousness which is actually your true self. You are actually that, who forgotten your own true self caught in the waves of ocean and storm.

That supreme consciousness is the one that creates, manages and absorbs everything in it. It has all required skills, expertise, power, authority and at the same time all its actions are performed under perfect harmony which is called "Yog". It is not Yoga of Asanas. Doing things, thinking, handling emotions, handling senses and keeping all ingredients of Anger, Lust, Passion, Greed etc in their own harmony and performing the actions as per the laws of Nature which is Dharma is THE MASTER ART OF ALL ARTS that exist in this cosmos. If that master art is known, the whole cosmos would be working for you. Any great thing can be done and achieved by man such as going to the moon, building some rockets and all, but man cannot just get this Master of Arts so easily.

Krishna is such Supreme Master of "that art" under whose control, all Natural forces and the unseen divine operational team work. He is that cosmic CEO who makes sure that order (Dharma) is followed all times, especially on the earth as human body is the best vehicle of transforming consciousness among all other beings.

That Supreme Being, who is always in harmony, his supreme art of all arts, always works with Arjunas to make sure that the order of things are in place. That Supreme Being is not a dead one, though he is not seen, but exists in the form of consciousness with energy. If you follow dharma well and tune to him at his frequency, you can perceive him.

In the world, everybody is in search of God. But the truth is God and he is always in search of Arjunas who always do their actions as per Dharma, the laws of Nature. God is after them actually, though they are not after him. Because of Arjunas alone, the world can be in order as per the laws of Nature. Else, it will always go topsy-turvy.

He always works with Arjunas and drives them, so that they can drive well, what they are driving!

CEOs basically drive the corporations and the corporations play very essential role in evolving the human consciousness. So corporations are very essential to be taken care by the Nature, the governance system of God.

Nature executes and performs various activities in the field of supreme consciousness (this world) to make sure that all souls sustain and evolve in it.

The Supreme consciousness again intervenes in the governance system of Nature when things go wrong. So he again looks out for Arjunas. Krishna when he lived on the earth, he needed only one Arjuna then to keep the Nature in order. But now, at this juncture of the world and its state, many Arjunas are needed.

Arjuna is not an ordinary one. He is master of various arts, perfectly skilled in what he does and stays always focused. Not just them, he by his Nature, falls in harmony with laws of Nature. He does not misuse his arts and show them off to gain applauses. He is someone who naturally has universal personality and does things out of compassion for the welfare of the people and the world.

Just like Keanu Reeves, Neil Anderson, in Matrix, does exceptional things, after knowing what is matrix! He does not quit what he is doing nor did he go to Himalayas.

When the secret of Matrix is known, then that GREAT ART of doing things will come that can perfectly be in harmony, all times. Then, you the CEO are hired by THE NATURE, THE MATRIX, to do its duty.

Its duty is not some secret job! It is the same job you are doing! But you will have all forces of

Matrix, The Nature with you always, when you become Arjuna.

Krishna, the supreme consciousness is ready to work with you and excel you in your actions. This book will help you tune to his frequency so you can take his help and perform great actions in your field of Business.

Chapter-4

The Purpose of Creation

The point of creation is an ever existing pure consciousness without any body. It always remains as consciousness without body. But, in order to experience itself in various body forms by giving free will to them, the consciousness splits itself into various limited consciousness particles that were born out of preliminary subtle elements such as mind, intellect, memory and subtle aspects of five elements and then the gross five elements. Objects that have life contain subtle elements of mind, intellect, memory and sensory elements and then they take the energies from the gross five elements to take the form of body which is actually the process that happens in the mother's womb in the first three months.

Objects that don't have life do not have all those subtle elements but purely form out of the gross five elements. Every object in the world is made of five elements in the world.

Just like the way you start your incorporation from a point of thought primarily and then, you process your thought in subtle fashion. You process your thoughts in terms of mission, objectives of the company, strategy, laws of operation, operation style and all. Then you bring them all into physical form by recruiting people and then you expand the operations in the physical form.

Before even thought, primarily, LOVE and DESIRE is the root of forming a company. The desire of doing something good, something helpful to the people is the basic reasons behind the formation of the company. Inherently if the desire is a good one, then it carries love and compassion within it. From there, the rest of the thought process in subtle fashion will start and then you bring them into physical form. You can compare this process of your company creation, with the process of the cosmic creation. Every object you think, in the mind has its subtle side of five elements. That is the evolution process of subtle elements into gross elements from there, the solid gross five elements turn into lifeless objects and living beings. Everything in the world including the living beings pull energies from the gross five elements and then only they can express themselves as objects.

This being the process, the primarily remembered point is to "experience its own self in various bodies"

To explain it in normal words, it is like; you give birth to your children. You see yourself in your children. For example, imagine, your son buying a car. Though you do not physically own it or though you do not drive it, you feel happy because, you feel as if, you own it. If your son marries you feel happy. If your children eat good food, you feel happy. You may not have the same food, but if your children eat good food, you feel happy. It is because, you see yourself in your children.

You do not feel such happiness, if a man on the road eats food. It is because, you gave birth to your children, you are emotionally attached to them and you see yourself in them.

In reality, you are also there in that man on the road. If he eats good food or if he owns a car, you do not feel because, you are not emotionally attached to him. But in reality, your consciousness is also there in him which you are not able to feel due to your awareness that is tying your consciousness to your body.

Coming back to the point of your children, creation "to see its own self in its split particles of consciousness", the creation took place. It is the same ultimate and supreme consciousness that is enjoying every good and bad moment of your life, being in the seabed of your consciousness. It's like having a small magnet in a big magnetic field. Small magnet would have its own small field of magnetism in the bigger magnetic field of bigger magnet. Your body is like that small magnet and your consciousness is limited like the magnetism of the small magnet. It is like that small magnetic field of yours, existing in the bigger magnetic field. You currently think that you are that small magnet, which is like your body. Your awareness is always tied to only your body. But you are that magnetism of it by reality. You also do not know that your body is existing in bigger magnetic field which is this whole cosmos. Again, that whole cosmos is not objects as you see. It is the largest and vast magnetic field of a big magnet. Actually there is no big magnet in physical form, but its magnetism is existing everywhere, in and out of every living and non-living things. That magnetism is nothing but the cosmic consciousness whom we all call, God and you have your own limited consciousness in it with your own body. Just like you took body with your own limited consciousness, incarnation of God takes place with that unlimited consciousness. If God comes down in human body, he would have that unlimited, huge consciousness in him with all its governance system, power and energies.

It is that universal consciousness and its energy that actually digests your food; it is that consciousness that logs out of your body system when you are asleep. It is that consciousness that gets charged out of your breath, because of which your body is able to function.

So, the bottom line is that single consciousness that is there in all living and non-living objects. It does, unseen works such as creation, sustenance and dissolution of the bodies. It also has two more main responsibilities such as concealing its true nature to keep all souls bound to the world and the fifth responsibility is revealing its true nature, which can be experienced by opening the inner eye.

The bodiless pure and supreme consciousness, keeps sacrificing itself in order to run the show of the creation. The creation was started just like an incorporation that is established. But in order to sustain it and manage it, the supreme consciousness keeps working in the background all times, which is its selfless sacrifice. Just like, when you were child, your father worked behind to keep you and all family members happy. As a child you were not aware of all his pains. Just like your father, when you have your own children, for their welfare, you sacrifice all your desires and interests and work hard.

The soul particles which actually came from the supreme father consciousness are required to go through the evolution of knowing their true-self in their entire journey of living. It means, firstly you should know that you are not body and you are that small limited consciousness and then you should also merge your limited consciousness in the supreme consciousness and know that you are that supreme consciousness itself. That means, their consciousness evolves by detaching itself from the body, its associated attachments and expands for its true identification. The journey includes several births and deaths. As part of their living process, the souls go through their desires, passion and the karma they owe to the world. Those desires and passion make them do their karma (work). The work they do sustains them in the world, while they go through the true-self-realization process. Is it not a life of evolution? Did your mind evolve since you took birth? If you look back five or ten years, are you the same man who made certain decisions poorly? Today, you make better decisions because you learnt out of your experience which is nothing but the evolution and expansion of yourself. In that process, you also get disciplined. You do not commit some mistakes that you committed few years ago. You do not commit them because you know that, if you do them again, you will have the pains.

The situations in life, the difficulties and pains make you realize that you should not repeat the mistakes done earlier. In that process, they keep realizing the mistakes and try to get more and more perfection through several births and deaths. Mistakes are nothing but the actions that are against the laws of Nature which produce the karma that result them go through pains and suffering. So, the man gets to know the mistakes which are nothing but the laws of Nature. But this understanding through practical situations is a quite long process which is a result of several lives of the souls. Some people act so disciplined at their young ages and they experience better results in their lives out of their actions. It is because; they practiced the disciplined life which is being in harmony with the laws of Nature in earlier lives. Because of that, their actions and talks appear to be so matured at their young ages.

The primary purpose of the whole creation is to get you know this, laws of Nature and how the Nature, the environment in which you are living, functions.

Even if you do not know about the laws of Nature, you can act in every situation by seeing yourself in others. Then you naturally fall in harmony with the laws of Nature.

However, it's the main purpose of the creation is to bring this transformation in the souls of knowing the true self which actually liberates them and take them back to the source of creation which further does not produce any births and deaths.

Knowing the true self or self-realization is like "evolution of an employee from a lower level to the CEO level". Meaning, imagine, an employee who started his career in your company from the lowest level of duties and imagine he grew through the entire corporate ladder and then imagine he becoming the CEO of the company. It is not an ordinary journey. It requires lot of commitment, sacrifice, understanding the whole business in all aspects, understanding not just the business, understanding the objectives and mission of the company etc come into picture. Apart from all those, personal sacrifice of reaching his objectives "of becoming CEO of the company" and going through all that discipline require lot of "love" for what he is doing. Starting such journey is easy but sustaining in that whole journey is quite difficult and requires lot of sacrifice in all aspects of life. Because it is a long journey, it requires continued encouragement and undying love for what he is doing.

But finally who can become CEO? He who understands the whole system of the company and whose consciousness is spread across the company, who is alert all times, he who fallows the laws, values and ethics of the company becomes the CEO. So, he who becomes the CEO gets to know the whole system of the company and his consciousness spreads across the company. In a way from his business perspectives, you can say, he is "self-realized" in knowing the entire system of the company. He, in his journey, gets so emotionally aligned with the company. He will start losing his own self and he starts identifying himself with the company itself. His identity of "Me So and So person" will be forgotten by that person and he becomes literally that company itself. He loses his personal self and identifies himself with the vast system of the company. At that state, If you ask him his name – he will say "I am so and so company". He will not mention his name. He will tell the name of the company. His consciousness expands and becomes vast with the identification of the company itself. This state of losing personal self and becoming "that vast true self" which further reveals the truth is nothing but the self-realization. After becoming self-realized of being CEO and knowing the entire system of the company and working for few more years, he gets relived from his desires of doing something in business, and there is nothing left for him to know in that incorporation. That is the state of getting released from the Karma. Meaning, after realizing this, he may work for few years and later, he may want to retire and be in peace or probably he will become the advisor for the company. His life will go on and he remains happy and in peace without doing anything. That is the state of freedom from all his desires of "doing that or doing this" and so on. He becomes desire-less and remains in peace in his own self. He achieves this unless until he further develops any other desires! Having achieved this state, most successful CEOs and entrepreneurs establish non-profit organizations and serve the world.

From the cosmic creation perspectives, knowing that entire system of creation in physical, mental and spiritual realms is nothing "realizing the self". Everyone starts the journey in knowing the truth but at the end, they get to know that, they are that truth!

Once his soul realizes that true self, then it will start losing all its desires and its karma starts getting null and thus he remains in peace without any desires and then he will be liberated from his bondages of the world.

There is another level on top of knowing the entire system of the creation. That is, becoming creation and creator itself. At that level, he even loses the identification of CEO and becomes that company itself. He becomes that creator and creation, who is there in all and in whom all exist.

Then, he can even control the whole creation and the governance system of the creation (which is Nature). This is highest level of realization. This happens very rarely and it is a rare divine occurrence.

If you observe the whole journey of this man becoming CEO, his mind, his intellect and his way of thinking, his way of talking, his way of functioning and working style keeps evolving and gets finer and finer, purer and purer and subtler and subtler. He gets to know the "FUNCTIONS OF MIND AND INTELLECT" and he knows the art of dealing with all stakeholders in a harmonious way. His works and actions would get more and more subtle. Meaning, as he grows in his corporate ladder, you find that his works are not exhibited externally and they are more subtle and not visible to all people in the company. As you know, the work of the CEO or the advisors of the board and their works would not be quite physical in terms of actions. But their actions play greater role in the mind, intellect and then take the form of verbal or little writing fashion. They play more of energy transmitters like football coaches in their team members who further function with his energy and vision in their corporations.

In the corporate ladder, everyone cannot become CEO from the lower level. Some grow to certain level and stop their evolution. But it is also required that some should stop in the middle of evolution.

Only Arjuna can become the CEO of a company. Arjuan is one of the five brothers of Pandavas, who is more skilled, sharp in mind and who only sees the target perfectly. On top of all those he carries the discipline, the dharma i.e. being in harmony with the laws of Nature and above all, he sees himself in all other living beings. He carries the attitude of fire and ice at the same time. He is chosen by Krishna the supreme consciousness to bring back dharma in the world. He further gets trained and his complete system is driven by the unlimited divine forces which gets Arjuna a great victory and the kingdom. That work of Arjuna and his victory is a never forgotten achievement in the history of the world. Arjuna and his works are always discussed by the men to inspire themselves, as long as this creation exists. Only such people would get ready to become CEOs. Then, such CEOs will be chosen by Krishna, the supreme consciousness to implement dharma in the business that gets right prosperity, expansion of business, name and several other things involuntarily. Though the Pandavas, the five brothers were unfairly given a drought field as their kingdom, Arjuna builds a phenomenal fort and kingdom with the help of all divine forces and Nature in a very short span of time. That work of Arjuna surprised all kings and people, those days. Arjuna could achieve all that, because of the DIVINE DRIVING FORCE of Krishna which worked in him. The same divine force works in CEOs, who could become Arjunas in businesses to do such phenomenal things through their incorporations. When Arjuna is ready and especially when Krishna the supreme consciousness drives him, all forces of Nature and divine forces would be with him to act and then Arjuna's actions would create phenomenal things in the world which world can never forget.

Coming back to the point of evolution, some employees who try to become CEOs from the lower levels would stop in the middle of their journey due to various reasons. If they do not stop in the middle, everybody will become CEOs. If everyone tries to become CEO, the lower level works in the company will not happen. Meaning, if all become CEOs, who will work in the lower levels of the company? They stop in the evolution process based on their desires and various other factors. Nature does not allow them to evolve beyond their own level of transformation by which they contribute to the world. Nature also stops someone at a certain evolution level, because it expects him to burn the balanced karma based on the level he achieves. Some would be interested to become only General Manager. So they would reach that goal and stop evolving further in the corporate ladder.

In the same way, even in the cosmic evolution, every soul will not try for self-realization.

This process of evolution, of becoming subtle is the soul evolution, in terms of cosmic creation.

As part of its operations, the creation, as part of its objective realization process, it gives all required infrastructure and cooperation for the souls in it to live. Without giving the platform to live, they cannot sustain and go through the self-realization process.

Creating is easy, dissolution of the creation is also easy, but in between the sustenance of the creation requires lot of management expertise. In order to run the corporations, CEOs cannot go out of the ways of Laws of Nature and do some actions and such actions will quickly bring back unexpected tsunamis that challenge the existence of their businesses. So in sustenance process, following Dharma, the laws of Nature, is very essential for the CEOs. For ordinary people also, the current life is a sustenance process in which they earned this body and it should be used to be in harmony with the Dharma so that they can evolve well and transform. Else, they also get into Tsunamis of karmas which will put them far behind in their evolution and earn them karma of pains big time.

So in its platform of womb, The Nature gives certain basic infrastructure and it also works behind in main functions of the bodies of living beings in an unperceivable way.

Nature gives an infrastructure (this world) of five elements for its inhabitants. All physical things we make in this world are the forms of five elements. So without the basic infrastructure given by Nature, we cannot even have a small pen made for us. In fact your body itself cannot exist without five elements. You cannot operate your life without the continued help of five elements. Apart from the physical world of five elements, Nature involuntarily manages the breath of all living beings (It is a life force that works like electricity to sustain the living beings). Without Nature's force, you cannot even drain out waste coming out of your body. Nature's burning force acts behind the action of digestion in all living beings. All organs in the body function with unperceivable actions of Nature. That force actually is the energy of force of the supreme consciousness. You can consider the example of weather to know this. If the weather is cloudy for few days, you do not feel hungry like the way you feel on sunny days. The field of Nature and its works exist externally to you and also internally in you.

Not just these works, in order to sustain people, Nature also meets employee-employer, buyer-seller, boyfriend-girlfriend and so on, as per their Karmas and desires. In your business, you can easily perceive the unknown force of Nature, especially in terms of the business opportunities and in certain crucial decisions.

These are all unperceivable actions of Nature working in a very subtle way through our subtle realms. Normal human with his naked eyes, cannot see these works. Inner eye is required to perceive all these subtle works of Nature. Your logical mind with individual ego, cannot accept these actions but yet, you are living in the pool of uncontrollable and unperceivable pushes and pulls of actions of the Nature. You are experiencing such forces in your daily lives, you are living by them, you are experiencing those actions and you are also feeling some of its benefits but yet, you do not give importance to these actions of Nature. Because, your mind is not that subtle to prove to others nor you have proof of its actions to show them to others. So you just live by its actions in an involuntary way and Nature does not need any applauds for its actions from you. It does its works automatically as per its algorithm.

The purpose of creation secondarily, is to sustain all the human souls mainly by showing them the place to work, where they burn their desires and passion. This being the secondary objective, its main objective is to lead the souls forward by burning their desires towards, knowing their true self that ultimately liberates them from their karma (of desires, passion and traits) and in that journey, their transformation expands their mind and help them see the world in its original way, so they do not accumulate karma further.

As part of this karma burning process, the souls go through happy movements, sad movements, pains, suffering etc. The experiences that come out of their personal karma are borne by their limited consciousness while the non-personal karmic experiences are enjoyed by the supreme consciousness which is there in the seabed of your personal or limited consciousness. That experience is enjoyed by supreme consciousness through various bodies of living beings, just like the CEO, feels himself in all employees and in the entire system of the company. It is him who feels happy if any employee does a great thing in his company.

So, from the corporate perspectives, what is THAT ONE which is the truth? It is only THE COMPANY that is truth. Your company is a field of energy with its own laws and objectives. That company is there in every employee of the company. You get to see the bodies of the employees and their names. But the truth is ONLY THE COMPANY that is in the hidden layers of every employee.

So from the subtlest truth perspectives, ONLY COMPANY is existing in every employee. So now the question is – what is company? Is it a body? Is it a building? Or is it a legal certificate of the company? You cannot physically identify the company in reality. So the truth is company is a system that cannot be seen by naked eye, heard by ears nor felt by touch, nor can be tasted or smelled.

The system can only be felt in the consciousness that includes mainly your mind and intellect. But it cannot be felt by the senses. So those, who have better consciousness, are only capable of knowing the system of the company.

It is an unseen subtlest system of Matrix. That system is there in every employee. The creator of the company exists ever after many years of his physical death. But the system of the company still goes on living and growing. The creator would always be existing in the subtle form behind the subtle system of the company. Just like Steve Jobs ways of doing things, being always with the system of the company, Apple. To perceive, that the company is a system, it requires subtlest mind and inner eye. I am sure after reading all this, you understand that the company is a system and to feel it, it requires inner eye and everyone cannot feel it. You can go to any employee and explain this whole thing and ask him, if he can feel that the company is an unseen subtle system. I am sure, he will not be able to answer, and he will even get bored if you explain this whole thing to him. So everyone is not capable of having the inner eye. In the same way, everyone cannot read this book!

Everyone is not capable of reading this book and those who are ready to become Arjunas can read and have the interest to read.

If you ask this question to few employees, most of the employees get bored in listening to this knowledge of the truth.

The truth is that in every company, CEO's consciousness and energy flows through the veins of the company. Veins does not mean the gross building pillars of the company, it is the minds of all employees. CEO may have one body in reality. But it is the CEO who has several bodies as shown in the picture below.

It is Lord Krishna whose supreme consciousness that is there in every living being and nonliving being of this biggest corporation called creation.

In the same way, a CEO's consciousness is there working in everyone indirectly in the company. But how active it is and how energetic it is, is what matters and keeps the corporation great in the world!

The lower employee may follow the instructions of his immediate boss. But he does not know that, those instructions actually come from the CEO of the company. So the CEO becomes an unseen action in the company. It is his energy of force that works behind the actions of the employees. Though the employees have their own WILL, their own ways and styles of working, the energy and force of the CEO remains in the subtlest layer of every employee that actually makes them work. Of course, it is the medium of Nature and its energies that actually are there in the background of CEO's energy.

That subtlest force of energy comes from the consciousness of the CEO who always thinks about his company. His mind space is totally occupied by the thoughts of his company always. So his thoughts, his soul energy, his all personality runs through the veins of the corporation which works as a force behind all employees. Currently that force does not work at greater degree, because the energy of the CEO's consciousness is limited.

So who is the actual doer behind everybody's positive action in the company? It is, in a way CEO's energy and CEO who is the main doer in the form of energy force. The same thing is applied in a larger scale to the creator of this universe.

Some employees get inspired by their CEOs and they all look up to him in their professions and lives. When they are inspired, they naturally think, act and behave like their CEOs. That means, they carry the energies of their CEOs and it is Nature that supports all such CEOs and their energies in the background.

The energies of CEO and his consciousness could become great if he has the forces of Nature with him, at the fullest level. A CEO can have the unlimited forces of Nature with him only when he becomes True Arjuna. When a CEO has forces of Nature with him, he can experience manifestation of his thoughts taking place in his business. He can easily observe people. They will work for him, out of love and interest and the results of their works would stand out in the company. At the end, all those phenomenal works, their greatness, their fame and all belong to the corporation. This book will lead you to the first level of invoking the forces of Nature and taking their help in your corporate works and they will only work if you have positive mind and positive intentions.

Going back to the presence of CEO, his actions are visible in various employees. Physically, all employees do not get to see their CEO. But his actions would work in deep layers of their system. All employees cannot get to see the CEO nor do they have the capability of perceiving his actions. In the same way, you as a normal man, without having inner eye, you cannot perceive the actions and works of Nature or the cosmic CEO. Cosmic CEO is even superior to Nature. Nature works for him and stands by him like unlimited energy of a governance system.

In the same way, this entire creation is a system. The creator is merged in the system. The creator is not perceived by your senses nor mind or by your intellect. You require inner eye to know his subtle works.

Every employee cannot get to see the CEO of incorporation. In fact all employees do not even try to meet the CEO. Some try and some who have better understanding of the business, some who perform well in the company, some who have subtle and better minds and behavior and character only get to meet the CEO.

In the same way, everyone will not try to know the creation and its subtle science.

- Some think of knowing it
- Some attempt to know it.
- Out of them, only some get into the journey of knowing it
- Out of them, only some can stand in the journey and many will quit
- Out of all those who remain, some fail at the end
- Out of them only very few get to know the truth
- Even out those truth knowers, only one gets to really become the system itself or creation itself. He is not seen any more with individuality. He is lost or merged in the creator, creation and becomes one with both creator and creation.

So, if you observe this process, if a thousand people try to know the creation and its science, only three will get to know it and only one really becomes the self or creation itself.

He gets to know that he is in all and all are in him and it is him alone in all. It does not mean, I am asking the CEOs to become that creator or creation by taking Himalayan route. My comparison of this is with the corporation.

When you, the CEO becomes Arjuna, with the help of the supreme consciousness who becomes your driving force can get you this vision of your true self being in all employees and in the system of the company itself.

So you as a CEO, will no more be a physical one, though you remain with a body, but the true self merges in ever living and non-living things of the corporation and by that unlimited force, a corporation can run involuntarily just like this big incorporation called "The Creation" runs. I am not saying some imaginary concepts.

Oh... The Arjuna Of future ....You will know as you keep reading this book further.

Chapter-5

Creation And Strategy

When you start incorporation, you would have your own strategy in the beginning to manage it. You would have your own algorithm that becomes the running machine of the company you establish. That algorithm becomes a kind of law for all the people to work in the company. It would have its own love, compassion that encourages the employees to work and at the same time it would have its own strict laws that work against them if they commit any mistakes. Every department of your company would have their own strategies that encourage employees and all associated partners to work together for the welfare of the incorporation.

In the same way, the creation has its own algorithm and strategy.

The supreme soul or the nucleus of the cosmos contains the main ingredients of consciousness such as Ego, will, awareness, intellect, mind, memory and also the subtle aspects of senses. These are the subtle aspects of the soul or consciousness. For the creator, those ingredients work for the welfare of the universe. The same contents are also there in all consciousness particles of the main supreme consciousness.

The strategy is that, the WILL which is given to the souls, is what separates them from the supreme soul. That WILL creates the separated EGO and makes the souls pursue their own desires, interests and preferences. The separated ego connected with desires, interests and preferences make them get into new karma and that karma makes them further get into actions and they further reap the karma again. That is how; they are caught in repeated fruits of their karmas or actions as they do not know as to how to do the action or karma. The life of every being is like a dream state in which they keep living. One day, they will wake up to know the actual science that this book reveals.

WILL is the strategy of the supreme soul that actually makes the soul particles to run the show of the creation. Unless they have their own desires, will, interests the show of the creation, will not happen and the material world will not evolve.

The WILL is like, say you are the CEO of the company and you hire some people to work for you. You define their work, laws of company, operational procedures and other terms and conditions. But yet, you give them free hand in doing their work. Free hand does not mean that they go against the laws of the company and harm the company. Within the given framework, they are required to perform using their mind, talent and skills.

That freehand is like, the WILL. You have given them the free hand. In order to perform well and get attention by the boss, one cannot harm other employees and do other unacceptable actions. Those actions must have not been mentioned in the laws and terms and conditions of your company. It is not possible to mention all laws and terms and conditions in the employee contract. They are called values, ethics and other terms as such, which are required to be there by default in human system. So, after committing some mistakes, the employees cannot say that "they are not mentioned in the contract so I committed that mistake". But inherently every soul knows what is right and wrong deep within, which is the true nature of every soul.

The laws of the cosmos also work the same way. Everything is not mentioned in a cosmic manual or contract given to its inhabitants. We all know that it is wrong to abuse someone on the road. Of course, for small mistakes, there are no laws in our countries. If someone abuses wrong words to you on the road and runs away, can you report to the police? You cannot report but yet, you know that it is wrong. For such actions, though you do not get any punishment from the police but the "laws of cosmos" do not leave you from the punishment of such actions.

Every man in the conscience knows that it is a wrong act. But yet some people do such actions. For such actions, the cosmos and its laws definitely give the punishment to its inhabitants. Those actions earn bad karma and one day or the other; the souls will go through the punishment of such actions. Out of such punishments they definitely suffer and go through the pain.

So, the WILL works like that. You as CEO have given free hand to the employees to work but it does not mean, they do some actions that are unacceptable. Then, for such actions obviously the employees face the consequences. The same rules apply to the CEO, the owner of the company as well, if he does the mistakes. He becomes the leader, who works and abides by the laws of the company, though he is the owner of the company. So, the free hand is like the "will" given, to the employees and it cannot be misused. It is given to work for the welfare of the company. It is not given to work against the company or to work as they want, in their own directions.

The same thing is happening with all souls in the world at this moment. They all work in their own directions by not knowing the actual objectives of the cosmos and the creation. It is like employees working in their own direction by not giving importance to the objectives of the company. Will such company grow or evolve? No right? In case of companies in the world, a company and its life is maximum looked at few decades of life and a little over it. But when it comes to the creation, its life is of millions of years and the evolution is a slow process that has several impacts. The evolution of creation is a biological evolution but not mechanical! So the evolution happens, cell by cell in all realms.

If every employee works in his own directions, the company cannot survive and the result can be known in few months or years in a large company. But the creation is a very huge system. The impact cannot be known in few years. The impact is known in few hundreds of years. Such time is given to the souls to mend their ways and transform in order to understand and cooperate with the laws of the Nature.

So, the strategy of the creation goes like this ...

- The will or free hand given itself makes the souls to have their own desires, aspirations, preferences, passion and so on.
- They further make the souls to do actions (karma) and that karma produces the material infrastructure to the world in which all the souls are living.
- That material infrastructure offers the facilities and comforts to the humanity. Bridges, transportation, medical technologies, computers, engineering and so on, are the fields in which the souls work out of their desires and passion that ultimately produce the material infrastructure and the comforts for the souls. This evolution of the world's infrastructure and comforts are directly connected to the souls and their evolution. All these actions they do, out of their

individual ego that binds them to the further production of new karma.

- As souls do not know how to do the karma, they connect their works to their bodies with their ego. The awareness of that body connection binds them to the new karma.
- That new karma again binds in new works. Those new works will further produce new karma.
- That way, the souls keep getting into actions and it is a process of few thousands of years of evolution.
- Just like logging into internet and logging out of it, the souls keep logging into the material world and logging out of it through several births and deaths.
- Every soul adds value to the infrastructure and comforts of the world. Either a man works as a carpenter or as a president of a country or as a great scientist, everyone contributes to the material world, including the one who cleans the floor in your office.
- The works they do, value add to the material world and evolves the material world. The wonder thing is that, from the same world, the souls logout (body dies) and again log into it, to enjoy the comforts and advancement of the material world. Unlike previous lives, they enjoy more comforts in their current lives and they further contribute to the world in their current lives.
- The explained evolution does not just belong to the human world; it also belongs to several other lives such as animals, creatures, reptiles, worms, germs,

plants and so on. But in the case of animals and all, they cannot work but they only are meant to bear their karma or pain and evolve.

- There are fourteen worlds as such for all the lives in the cosmos through which the souls evolve.
- Just like a trainee in your corporation, how he evolves and climbs the corporate ladder, in the same way, the souls evolve through various lives and finally end up with human life to speed up their soul evolution. Humans can well make use of their apparatus such as mind, intellect, awareness, ego, senses and so on. So they gain better soul energies while they live and evolve their souls faster, unlike any other species. They have the capability to make use of their apparatus much better. They usually just make use of their apparatus just around five percent of their potential. If they can make use their apparatus well, they can unearth many of their cosmic potentials to evolve much faster and try to get out of the bondage of the world which is the cycle of births and deaths. In that process, they can greatly add value to the world in a manner that humanity can never forget them. Those unearthed potentials not only evolve their souls but also greatly add value to them in their businesses and lives. As part of awakening those potentials, they also see great prosperity in their personal lives and businesses.
- In addition, the creation has Nature, which acts as the governance system with authority, power, energy and laws.

- Nature acts as a show hosting agent that gives required basic subtle infrastructure to the souls. The subtle works of Nature its infrastructure are giving five elements, Sun, Moon, Life Force management (because of which all bodies live), meeting the souls to their karma, breath management, logging in and logging out the life force during sleep etc. These are the basic subtle infrastructural elements that Nature as a host provides a living platform to the souls. In this platform or the world, the souls live, perform, contribute to the world and they evolve.
- Nature also carries set of laws which is called The Dharma. Those rules can never be documented or even if they are done to certain extent, they cannot be remembered by the souls out of their mind in every situation. The souls know by default in their consciousness about these laws, provided they touch the bottom layer of their consciousness. But they can never touch this bottom layer, because of their diseases such as anger, lust, jealousy, hatred, cheating others, lying and many other traits. So they most of the times go against the laws of Nature and then they get into karma which they further have to bear.

The root strategy to run the corporation of the creation is “free will” given to the souls. That itself makes the souls go through millions of years of evolution. So the life of the creation-incorporation is of several millions of years. Its main management energies are creation, sustenance and dissolution. Souls fall in the trap of free WIL given, which they use and start separating from the universal consciousness. Then the souls start getting after desires and get trapped for few thousands of years of lifespan by having bodies. Those bodies just cannot be of humans, they even fall down from that high level human consciousness to much lower levels to taking the bodies of various animals and so on. Imagine, the soul life span is of few thousands of years in various bodies which itself is a kind of life span of this creation. Then you imagine such life span of millions of souls, which is a huge life span of this whole creation. Now you can understand that strategy of giving free WILL that made the creation to continue its cycle for millions of years, which is nothing but the life span of the "incorporation of the creation".

This strategy makes the whole creation a self-sustaining and self-managed incorporation in an automatic algorithm that always runs.

Some of these souls, will turn out to be so negative in the process of their thousands of lives. They become part of the negative energy of the cosmos.

So, now you see the evolution of energy being split into positive and negative sides of the cosmos which work like push and pull energies to balance the whole creation and sustain in its life span. Both positive and negative energies came out of the initial cycle of creation. Now this negative energy adds value in increasing the LIFE SPAN of the whole creation or cosmic incorporation. Because, as the positive energies take forward, negative energies pull behind the whole progress of the creation and the rift between them makes it a longer show. There are positive and negative cosmic management teams that work by souls and they manage their domains, who have bodies. Domains do not necessarily to be geographical locations but based on the transformation of souls in terms of negativity and positivity.

The positive cosmic management team has higher energies due to their level of universality. Their evolution rate is much higher in comparison with negative team, but they are not fully transformed divine souls. The positive cosmic team is also required to evolve and go beyond their current statuses and merge in the nucleus of the cosmos which ends their soul evolution process. It means, they can advance and at the same time, they can also fall down from their status of being the cosmic management team members due to their bad deeds. Imagine, Sun, not doing his job properly for few days. Imagine the same kind of bad performance of duties from five elements, clouds, oceans and so on. Obviously there would be a huge disturbance in the whole nature and atmosphere in which we all live. Then, such deeds earn them big time karma by which they fall down from their status of cosmic management team members and they will take up the form of human bodies and then they further evolve in human form. They can gain back their position if they do good deeds as humans. Till they come back, some other energy will be given their responsibility. Even positive divine energies can fall down in their evolution because, they also carry certain "traits" that are imperfect in terms of universal consciousness. When they do not perform their duties properly, they are blamed by negative energies and negative energies try to invade the positive energies. Now you see the balancing that is brought due to push and pull activities of both positive and negative energies?

The negative energies based on their negativity, they are spread everywhere in all realms of the creation. The lower levels of creation belong to reptiles and beyond them where dark sides of actions take place. Life there is so hard. Mostly positive energies and its team members manage cosmos, performing their duties in a positive way. The opportunity of ruling the cosmos is given to both positive and negative teams. The positive cosmic management team is given three fourths of time span of one creation, while the negative energies are given one fourth time of opportunity to rule the world. But the negative energies always try to invade positive energies and try to reduce their ruling span of time. Due to this push and pull rift between positive and negative cosmic energies, the life span of the creation sustains quite longer.

If you take the example of a story, you call it a story because there are always some situations in the story in which all people act. Isn't it? If there are no situations, if there are no disturbances, pushes and pulls in the story, the story will not last longer and the story also does not look interesting. Imagine, if there is no requirement of your customer arises, you will not get work. Imagine, if some of your team members do not perform well and do not do good job in a project. Imagine that is not observed by both your company and the client. So, that bad job is underlying danger like a bug which might erupt anytime. That eruption further creates more work for you and your company which brings more money and increases the project life span. But the point is, that bad job doer, will anyway gain his karma which makes him one day suffer in a big way. However, the sustenance of you, your company and your team is increased due to that bad job weather it was done intentionally or unintentionally. This is just one case that explains to you, how the life span of the SHOW increases due to both pushes and pulls in the story. The bad job gets exposed when it reaches its brimful level in terms of Nature. Then both companies might take some action on them or both companies might end up their relationship which ends the story. But the CEO and the top management will always jump in, to not to end the story. They apply all their energies constructively to continue the story. In terms of creation, the story does not end so easily, how worse ever dangers might erupt in the story of creation, the CEO and Nature of the creation makes sure that, some solution is found which sustains the creation.

So that is how this saga of creation keeps happening for millions of years. All souls again and again go through their karma and do various works. That karma makes them dream and produce more desires and passion. Then they further work and in the process of doing that work, as they do not know how to perfectly do the karma, they will again accumulate new karma out of their bad deeds. So the story of the creation goes on like this.

To this entire story of creation, push and pull actions of positive and negative energies further add FUEL to the FIRE of free WILL given to the souls. This again increases the lifespan of the whole creation.

But one thing that no one can avoid in the whole creation is, evolution. Weather they belong to positive or negative sides, they are required to evolve. They may either advance or fall from their current state. Meaning, a negative soul can evolve to be a positive soul and further it can evolve from human consciousness to much advanced state of playing a role in the positive cosmic management team.

The current juncture of the creation is that last, one fourth span, in which the ruling is given to the negative energies. So their style of work is totally opposite way to the Nature. Negative energies always carry weaknesses, they give importance only to their bodies and they use less of their mind and intellects. They are so lazy and they are used to alcohol and all those intoxicants including the sexual enjoyment and so on. They are always greedy, filled with ego for power, authority, money and possessiveness. Deception, lust, greed, over anger, controlling others, binding others, being like parasites, high end of showoff and all are part of their Nature and the list goes on like this. They never believe in god, discipline and all those. They believe in taking spiritual energies from negative forces. So they do such rituals and spiritual practices that gain them negative energies. So you can imagine, the kid of management they do, if they get into the power. They obviously promote and inject their negative nature to the world. The ruling came into their hands because of their extreme negativity such as being born out of sister-brother relation. So you can imagine the kind of negativity the current ruling management in cosmos has and the kind of negativity it would inject into the human consciousness. Their negativity also increases day by day in Nature and reaches its brimful level. You can read how they inject their negativity into you.

For example, you need some kind of discipline in life to grow and sustain right? Say you are a senior executive in your office and you obviously would have some discipline and leadership qualities in your personality which are positive. But when the negative energies take over the ruling of the cosmos, they work against the discipline. They try to introduce and inject indiscipline and bad habits in your system. Some friends come to you and they probably introduce you to drugs and so on, that will put you out of discipline. You may simply taste them initially and experience them. But later it becomes a habit and then you go indiscipline in your life. You do not go to office on time, you do not perform well, you might misbehave in the office out of drug intoxication and then your downfall will start. Finally one day, you will lose your job. You might even loose good relations in your personal life. So, basically you are introduced to the negative habits that totally crushed you in your life professionally, emotionally, financially and by health. Introducing NEGETIVITY is the great work of the current governance system of the cosmos. They want to crush all humanity. They slip negativity into your system so sweetly and smoothly through the doors of your weaknesses.

The negative governance system wants everyone to be in intoxication of senses i.e. being into drugs, being into over alcohol drinking, over smoking, doing prostitution, intoxication of power, money, and authority and so on. All these will totally make you more egoistic and make you function out of over anger, over authority, ruling or controlling others, being greedy of money by harming others and so on. You find people carrying all these traits such as jealousy, possessiveness, insecurity, anger, having authority, controlling others, winning over others, covering mistakes, showing off the talent or performance, even falling to a level of doing mean actions. All these, you find in today's offices. In which office you do not find these?

These are not the actual characteristics of the people. They are involuntarily influenced by the current negative ruling system of the cosmos. Their characteristics are meant to totally destruct you, your environment, your company, your society, your country and the world. The negative management system does not want the creation to be in prosperity. They want all to suffer, to be in pain and that is what gets them the happiness and enjoyment. The intoxication the negative energies induced into your system might appear to be good temporarily but they are like a slow poison, meant to destruct you.

You know that the government in your country has unlimited authority and power. Just like your government sustaining based on the taxes you pay, Nature also sustains based on the evolution of the souls in its womb. Nature has unlimited energy that it gets from its nucleus but however, it has its limits in sustenance based on the energies that it receives from its contents (the souls that live in its womb),

If the negativity increases, you basically go out of discipline and you do not pay taxes to the government. In the same way, if the negative energy increases in the Nature, the production energy goes down. Production of energy happens from within the system i.e. out of the souls within and if they go against the laws of Nature, obviously Nature would get imbalance. Then the system demands CEO of the incorporation to jump into the situation and do some firefight for the sustenance of the incorporation. He is required to bring balance in the whole incorporation. He initially sends various authorities of his to bring balance in Nature and when the situation goes worse, then he jumps into the situation directly.

So, in short, to say, to manage this entire creation, Nature and algorithm, there are several cosmic energies that work in the form of souls and they can be called as “positive cosmic management team”.

You will be introduced to these energies on the cosmic aspect and also on the soul particles aspects (which is you, your incorporation etc), in the next chapter.

Chapter-6

Cosmic Management Team

There is a huge cosmic team of divine souls, in the cosmic incorporation of creation, whom you cannot experience by your senses. It requires using the abilities of subtle energies to perceive them. They remain in the soul form and do their universal duties of cosmic incorporation.

To simply understand, you can think of the Sun. Sun is not a dead physical thing that you see and you cannot argue out of physical world as well because, Sun emits unlimited energies and heat that requires for the atmosphere of the whole cosmos. Earth is just one of the planets in the whole cosmos in which you are just one of the living beings out of many. Sun is doing his job burning himself all times, just like you. You also burn out yourself while doing the work you owe to this cosmic womb, but you burn for your limited personal gains. Sun is not a physical thing that you see but there is a soul behind it that does this duty of burning all times for the welfare of the cosmos. Sun is just one of the cosmic management team members. Rain, Seasons, Moon, stars, planets, five elements, oceans, clouds, mountains are some of such visible cosmic team members to your senses. There are several millions of such cosmic team members working in the soul form silently, behind the huge incorporation of this creation. I have only mentioned some of the team members whom you can perceive in the physical world by your senses. There are others, whom you cannot perceive by your senses. You need more subtle apparatus of your consciousness to perceive them.

In the cosmic management, both positive side of cosmic team and negative side of cosmic team participate in doing their jobs.

The positive cosmic management team has a boss and they also have a preceptor who is called the Guru.

Just like that the negative cosmic management team also has a boss and they also have a Guru.

They not only play their own cosmic roles given, but they also have major impact on the human consciousness mainly, as human body is the best vehicle for soul transformation. Humans, based on their positive-negative thoughts, emotions and actions, they generate certain vibes on which both negative and positive cosmic management team members have impact. By thoughts, emotions and actions a man can become conductive to carrying either positive or negative cosmic energies. By their vibes which work like antenna they can transmit the cosmic energies through them. If a man is more negative, he is supported by negative management team of souls, who will pump more negativity into that man and influence him to do negative actions. Especially when a negative man gets intoxicated, in his intoxication, he would have high influence of such negative cosmic forces. Then, he would totally loose his control and do negative actions such as crime and all. Many people carry negative emotions and thoughts in their minds but yet they do not commit negative actions because of the fear they have about the legal actions. But when they get intoxicated, that fear will be overcome with the help of the negative forces and their energies that act on him. Those energies would influence and push him into committing crime. Once his intoxication goes down, he wonders if he did that crime on his own. That's the state of human today. Human by default is not that negative but due to the influence of negative cosmic forces, he becomes more negative.

Actually negative forces are meant to manage the dark worlds in which reptiles, cruel animals and all live. But as the current time and space (era called kaliyuga) is given to negative management to rule, they have more influence on the human world with all their negativity. Positive divine energies cannot do anything except watching all the negative management and its actions. They can only act, when they are invoked strongly or called by the humans.

But today, all humans have gone away from their religious or spiritual or yoga practices and they do not go through any discipline in life nor do they have any energy on their own. They are not mentally ready to accept any unperceivable cosmic energy. Out of, fake modernization mask, they are actually increasing their weaknesses and through those doors, these cosmic negative forces are slipping into their systems and influencing them to commit some bad actions. I am sure; you must have seen several people, whom you do not believe that, they could have committed some serious crime. All those are actually the influential actions of the negative forces in Nature through human bodies. The current negative management is making humans more and more conductive to carrying their negative energies, so they attract humans by showing taste of bad habits such as getting drunk, doing drugs and many other things.

The Gurus on both sides also play a role in the cosmos that demand them to show proper direction to their sides. But the point is, even if they show the right directions, the team members do not listen to their Gurus and get into wrong actions that harm the whole Nature and the world.

Above these positive and negative sides of cosmic management teams, there are three chief executives. They are creation, sustenance and dissolution energies. They rule and bring balance in both sides of management teams. It is their responsibility to bring balance in Nature but yet, they leave THE

FREE WILL to all souls in cosmos including that of both management teams.

They are top passive management team, like army bosses of a country. Army bosses, have all powers and they can control all the country, but the governance is given to a president of a political party who rules the country. Even if the politicians of the ruling party commit any mistakes, the army generals cannot take any action. But they will take action, if the government fails. Just like in the world, when the governments fall suddenly, armies take over the ruling till the next government is chosen by the people.

Especially the second energy in the top management is THE MANAGEMENT ENERGY that acts like a CEO to manage the whole cosmos, watches the show of the active management and when the nature goes out of its control, he comes forward to act. One of his acts is restarting the work with top four classes in the human society. One of them is the business class. To bring balance in human consciousness, as part of his divine efforts, he is trying to reestablish the connectivity with CEOs and entrepreneurs. This book is such efforts of cosmic CEO, VISHNU, carrying cosmic CEO energies.

Do not think the above said is like a story. It is the system within you and it is what is happening within you. Do not think, it is a system in the cosmos. What is there in cosmos, is there in you. What is there in you, is there in the cosmos. If you see the pomegranate fruit, you see seeds in the fruit and the same seeds can germinate, grow as a tree and again give fruits. The essence of the cosmos or the nucleus of the cosmos is there in you and you are there in the cosmic nucleus. You may call that Nucleus as God. Because you are technically like that pomegranate seed in the fruit that again has a seed within, you can act like that cosmic CEO in your business, provided, you work as per Dharma and take the help of Nature.

You can easily compare the above said with your own nature and system. You have both negative and positive traits within, which are ruled by their own energies. Those traits basically make the way of your life and those energies control you. You are not able to control those energies and the energies of those traits control you which is the reason why, you at times behave good and at times bad. You are like a puppet of your own energies within.

You in your life, always go through, creation, sustenance and dissolution actions out of all works you do. In a big way, establishing a company is like creation, sustenance of it is like managing it all times to make sure the business runs successfully and expands. When the company does not do well obviously it gets closed. This view is from the company perspectives. But this view applies to all small works you do in your daily life. You may be given a task by your boss which you start, sustain it and end it by submitting the work to your boss. Some jobs could be of few minutes to hours and some jobs could be of days and months. But the main job from the company perspectives has a larger duration of many years and decades together.

But the point is how these team members of the cosmos perform? They perform out of their own free will but at the same time, follow their duties as per the laws of Nature and definitions of their jobs. In terms of cosmic management team members, they gain the energies from the Nature. Both positive and negative management sides gain the energies from the Nature out of Tapas. Tapas is a sansrkrit word which you can call as discipline or a practice that lets you expand your consciousness. You can simply call it "consciousness management technique". Both sides of cosmic management team members go through this tapas by following the dharma (laws of nature) and perform their duties perfectly.

But the point is, who is technically giving the energies to them? It is the Nature which is giving energies to them. Because of its given energy they are able to perform their duties. But the way of performance of comes from the Nucleus or the supreme CEO. They gain that art of performing their duties in harmony. It is that harmony that gets them the energy. If the energies are not given, then obviously they cannot perform their duties. The Tapas practice alerts them to this truth that they are just being "vehicles in doing their cosmic jobs" and the actual doer is that cosmic CEO and his consciousness that is working through them and that is taking the energy from Nature and performing its duties.

So they know this truth and they can keep their ego in a balanced way and perform their duties. It is like though the Sun does his job, he won't pompously exhibit his pride out of ego. Technically he is shining because, he is getting the consciousness from the cosmic CEO and the energy from the Nature. He will miss the balance if the ego trips. Then, he misses the balance in his system, which makes him commit some mistake and that bad karma will slip him down from his current state. Just like some employee in your company if he starts showing off his performance and if he goes out of balance, then obviously, boss would not like it and such employee might get out of the job.

This TRUTH is known to all cosmic team members. As this truth is known to the cosmic management team members, they despite their great skill, talent and hard work, their pride associated with the performance and their ego does not take its exhibition form.

In the same way, in your company, though an employee has lot of talent, skill and works at free hand, the energy that comes to him is from the Nature. But the route of receiving the energy of Nature is the company and the top boss or CEO whose directions, vision and encouragement he follows. So in a way, that energy of the CEO is there in the system of every employee across the incorporation. So that has a very subtle role in the success behind the performer. Technically in the cosmic management team, the CEO of cosmic incorporation is so selfless and it is his energy that works through Nature and then reaches the cosmic team members.

Technically, the CEO of the worldly incorporation also falls in the same category of the CEO of the whole creation. But almost all CEOs do not meet the complete personality of the cosmic CEO. If they meet his personality even to a little extent, then the consciousness of such CEO and their energy spreads across their whole incorporation and gets quite bigger achievements.

But in real world, it does not work this way. Performance, talent, skill, hard work boosts the pride and ego of the doer and he starts exhibiting them. Such exhibition of pride and ego is encouraged in the corporations and in the society today. The truth is, the ego of the doer, is supported to encourage him so that the doer performs well. But imagine if his ego goes out of balance, then he will start acting in a funny way doing several other mistakes that are not acceptable by the laws of your company or the society or by the laws of Nature

Going out of the balance of ego, does not happen with just employees but also happens with the CEOs and hence, their quality of characteristics, consciousness and energy fall down and they get limited in all aspects of the duty and life.

Of course, the boss has to recognize such great skills, talent and hard work of the performer encouraging him tangibly in terms of monetary aspects and also in terms of educating him with true knowledge. If the CEO educates the employee in terms of his cosmic presence, then such CEO becomes the true leader and plays an active vital role in the cosmos management working for the cosmic CEO. That work may not happen directly from a CEO but can be through any other specific departments of the company. There will be a book shortly available, meant for professionals.

But primarily, it is the BOSS who has to walk the path of perfection in all aspects of profession and show practically to the down level executives and employees. It is the work of Rama who actually was like a leader with great universal personality. With the help of universal energies he could make a huge army of apes to cross the ocean and fight with Ravana. Such army members could even be ready to sacrifice their lives for that leader. Despite being an incarnation of God, Rama did not give any spiritual lectures. He showed the way of protecting Dharma, being in harmony with Dharma (The laws of Nature) right in the middle of the war. That war zone itself is a zone of life which includes even business. The actions of Rama were nothing but the examples set for the Man to follow the Dharma in the middle of chaos and war zone of life and business.

It needs lot of sacrifice, discipline and Tapas (the consciousness management practice) and following the Dharma (laws of Nature) in the business and life. Then, the whole cosmic energies work behind such CEOs who can even move mountains.

So it is the boss, who stands up first who has to be looked up by all employees in a natural way, out of his "personality", formed of above discipline said. Then the consciousness of such boss spreads across his cosmos (his incorporation) and behind that, the unlimited cosmic energy of Nature stands and works all times in all aspects of business and life. Then, many people work for such CEOs out of love, probably even without giving any money.

That is how the CEO of the cosmic creation, Lord Narayana works. He took ten incarnations so far on the earth to save the creation, especially human consciousness, from various dangers. He always practically lived up to the Dharma, the laws of the Nature with all characteristics and practices said above. The owner of the cosmic incorporation does not need to show off his pride because all members of the cosmos are just his own self.

It does not mean every CEO is expected to be, on par with the incarnating characteristics of the supreme consciousness or god. But if they could be met even to a little extent, it brings a lot of value addition not just to their businesses but to the whole Nature which is a bigger incorporation. Then, such acts definitely give some great benefits to the CEOs and his businesses.

In the CEOs who meet the cosmic frequency, this book will awaken such universal personality and introduce them to some practices and techniques that could be followed in life easily.

Remember, your company is not just some company that belongs to this world, but it is playing a cosmic role in Nature to advance the souls and in that cosmic work, you as CEO, are playing a great role.

So everything boils down to personality that is tied or expanded. It means, in technical terms, it is about "being detached or attached and being selfish or selfless. Being universal with cosmic power or being limited personal with very limited energy. That's what defines the line between Arjuna and normal CEO. As you keep reading this book, you feel the longing of your consciousness for its true expansion, which is its true Nature. Even if some fears are there in the background of the mind, your deep down keeps reminding you, its true nature!

Chapter-7

Position of Your Business In Cosmos

This whole creation is a selfless business of experiencing its true self of universal self and for its sustenance, this whole drama of business is managed all times. It is a selfless business in which the CEO of it just experiences his holistic self being in all beings. That business and its manager, the CEO sustains it and manages it for millions of years.

Business the word itself is meant "the place of burning the desires and passion" of souls. Work or profession related matters more occupy in our minds and that is what for every soul burns continuously.

Business ultimately drills down to giving some service to others. It is the service that you do to others, makes your body sustain for living.

Though we all have families, relations, parties, entertainment and various other things in our lives, still the profession or the work that soul longs for and it is what always there in the mind and the soul. Human mind is more occupied by the work related thoughts, though at times, our minds are occupied by other personal and temporary problems. But most of the times in life, the mind is occupied by work, its associated desires and its passion. That desire and passion for the work is the burning of the soul, which adds value to the whole creation. Meaning, every soul burns its karmas by doing their work and that is when their karma gets reduced. That karma is what you owe to this whole creation. After realizing your work alone, your soul satisfies. A carpenter after doing a good job, he feels satisfied, a film maker after making a good film feels satisfied, a software developer after seeing the function of the software, feels happy. A painter, by seeing his work, feels satisfied, an entrepreneur by setting up a business that keeps the customers happy, makes him feel satisfied. A house wife, after cooking food for her children, feels happy by seeing the happiness in them. All jobs have monetary results. But the work of a house wife does not get any monetary result. But it does not mean she is not doing her job. Unless your mother or wife cooks for you, you do not go to school or job and perform. The root cause for your performance is the job and love of the house wife and thus her value addition is much greater in terms of her energy and love that actually makes you perform well in your profession. So a housewife burns her soul and traits like that, dedicatedly for the welfare of her family. A father works hard to raise his children and burns himself for the welfare of his family.

After doing some works or working in a profession for some time, at times, people change their professions. It is due to completing the Karma that they owe to the world. They develop new desires or already remained desires arise from their soul system and then, they will run after realizing those new desires. After realizing and feeling satisfied or after getting bored out of old profession they take up new profession. They do not feel like continuing in their old profession. It is due to the completion of the karma they owe to the world. The traits related to that old profession would totally get erased from their system. Due to that, they feel satisfied and get bored with the old profession. Then they take up new profession. Changing jobs or moving to new companies at times happens due to the karma you owe to that place or company completes, so you move. There is a subtle work of Nature behind your actions. You will understand the subtle works of Nature in the forthcoming chapters.

Due to developing new desires that they store in their system for some time, they develop new karmas. So everyone, while doing their karmas that they owe to the creation, in that process, they further accumulate more karmas as some of their actions are done out of their personal self which is full of attachments or desires. The personal self is made of personal desires, personal preferences, fears, fear of losing, filled with personal expectations, insecurity, not having belief on the work you know, not doing the work out of the love for the work, being impassionate about the work, simply doing the work for temporary survival and so on. All these are the limitations related to ingredients of the soul that tie them to your limited self or body, which is made of all those disorders.

To sustain your business longer is also a part of cosmic management's responsibility. Your business is actually supported by the cosmic energy. Your business is giving platform for several souls where they burn their desires and passion for the work. That way, the souls can burn their karmas. Burning the karmas of the souls is the ultimate objective of the cosmic management. When the souls burn their karmas, they get rid of the obligated karma they owe to the cosmic womb or to this world or to the Nature. Then, their minds, their consciousness expand and get out of this cage or womb of the Nature. That is how a soul, merges back in its source of universal consciousness. That is what is freedom or liberation to the soul. That is when the soul actually attains peace. Till then, no soul attains actual peace. When a soul is in peace, that is when, The Nature, the womb also gets in peace. Till then, it is like the womb is bearing the weight of all souls.

Because your business is giving a platform to the souls to burn their karmas, your business is actually playing a cosmic role. Your business is indirectly helping the cosmos or Nature to evolve.

Your business is not just helping souls spiritually, but also giving the required money to the souls so that their material lives are taken care. Bodies are required for the evolution of the souls. So your company is actually doing a cosmic job in evolving the souls in both spiritual and material aspects.

Not just that, the third aspect of your company in doing the cosmic job is helping the material world to evolve in terms of its infrastructure.

So your company helping the souls to evolve spiritually, but also helping them to sustain physically and thirdly your company is improving the world and its infrastructure by providing your services and products to the world. So, now you understand what kind of cosmic job your business is doing to this world? It is actually not a selfish, limited and personal business. It is more than that and your business is more important to the Nature than you. So Nature's energies and also the unseen cosmic management teams are meant to work behind your business to support it.

If that is the cosmic role that your company is playing, imagine what kind of importance the Nature gives to you, the CEO. The whole governance system of the cosmos, the divine cosmic souls are meant to support CEOs like you, by their universal energies. But there is a condition in between that is totally stopping the businesses and the CEOs from getting the support of cosmic energies. That condition is meeting the condition of DHARMA in business. When it is met, the whole cosmos stands with you and your business.

There are few world famous companies that lasted more than 100 years. The reason behind their sustenance is the support of Nature. That means, their management followed the laws of Nature in managing their businesses at their best level.

So, your company is playing a big role in the whole cosmos, in not just from the cosmic sense of burning the karmas of souls, but also in the holistic economy of the world.

Your customers pay money to you, your customers' customers pay money to your customers. Your customer companies pay salaries to their employees. Your customer companies pay money to your company. You further pay salaries to your employees and they further pay their bills and sustain several other small time businesses and individuals through their lives. In this whole process, several people, their families are surviving. All this is a whole chain of sustenance game of the material bodies and they exchange money as per their karmas. It further causes social differences based on economy. Some are rich who have better comforts in life while others have low comforts and some do not even have any comforts in their lives. The money flows as per Karma and this work of Nature is unseen and it can never be perceived by normal humans in the whole background.

You are required to know about the play of the NATURE in this whole environment of the world, in which all companies, all living-beings and non-living things exist.

I am sure you know the seeable cosmic work that is happening in this environment of Nature where you get to see the work of Sun, the clouds, the work of five elements and so on. But beyond this physical work that you can sense by your senses, there is a universal work done by the Nature in the background which is like moving force behind the bodies of the souls so that they get to meet various bodies (people and other living beings) and situations, which is a hosting job of the Nature. The Nature which is the place and environment we all live in, has a job and its job is being HOST. It is the job of host that makes sure of giving required basic infrastructure and other basic needs for the souls so that they can perform their karmas in the environment of Nature.

The hosting energy of Nature is majorly working not just behind the souls but also behind every entity in the cosmos. From that sense, that hosting energy is also working behind your incorporation in a big way. Simply to say, there are so many companies working in the same industry. There is lot of competition. If you go to some streets in cities, you find lot of restaurants in the same street. But most of them survive. How do they survive?

There is a hosting energy of Nature working behind all our existence that is responsible for our survival. Because, our survival is connected to a huge chain of souls that again survive depending on us.

Everyone thinks they are just individual ones who are living their lives simply for their survival, thinking about just our sixty or seventy years of life. Some of us do not even see and recognize the universal entities such as Sun, Sky, Clouds, Five Elements and so on. Such disconnected way of personal lives most of us are living, without recognizing these cosmic natural forces.

So every individual and the companies need to understand their existence from the cosmic perspectives which is the truth. After understanding it, people can function by the fundamental required aspect of living life and running businesses, which is responsibility or Dharma. By following it, every individual and companies can get the help of Nature in all aspects of life and businesses that gives true prosperity.

Not just talking but rather, awakening the souls by energy to the awareness of integrated universal consciousness is the main purpose of this book.

Before all, you need to understand what is this Nature and its works, which is hosting all the living beings and non-living beings in its womb. You need to understand the way of living life in its environment so that we can gain success and prosperity involuntarily.

Chapter-8

The Nature

Nature does not mean those plants, mountains, weather and all. Technically Nature means, the mind, the traits, the emotions, the intellect, subtle energies behind the senses and the sense organs.

Imagine the trait called Jealousy. You carry jealousy to certain extent in your personality. Jealousy is not just a dead trait. It also carries certain energy. When situation comes, you will show the energy to the other people out of Jealousy and based on your energy level, other people would even take what you say, even if they do not like it. Others can't face you nor confront you because of its negative energy. Imagine there are several people in the world and everyone carries the trait called jealousy in them and they all carry the energies of that trait at various degrees. But if you take Nature as a whole, in the holistic sense, if you consider Nature as a dish, imagine the taste of the ingredient of Jealousy like salt, if salt is properly balanced in dish then it tastes good. If it is less, the show in Nature does not run well. Show of the creation has to go on right? Like a drama. To run the show, you need jealousy which is one of the main ingredients in the personalities of the Nature. If that salt element is more, then obviously the dish gets spoiled and the dish gets out of balance. The main point you need to understand is, not just the taste of salt but it has some energy. If the energy is more of a specific ingredient for example salt in this context, then that energy can damage the whole Nature or the world. Even though, jealousy, anger, lust and all are bad for the personalities, they are required to be there in their balanced levels so that you do your daily works well. If certain ingredients are less or more, then there will be imbalance in your personality and in the way you work in the world.

Yogis go beyond by leaving all these traits because they do not have anything else to do in life, like you. In the womb of Nature you owe back to the world big way, unlike Yogis. Yogis owe to the Nature very little. So they do not carry any responsibilities like you. They do not need any of these traits to manage their life because they do not have to go to office like you nor do they have any families to take care etc. Even if some Yogis have, Nature will somehow arrange required finances etc. for such Yogis and their families to live their lives.

But whereas you, and all people in the world, you all go to the offices and have various responsibilities, so for you the important thing is balancing these ingredients or traits in your personality, but not totally removing them or erasing them from your personality like a Yogi.

Balancing them is more difficult than just totally living in them or by just totally leaving them. It is just like your CEO job, walking on the razor edge. If you do not walk properly, you may slip either side.

Nature's objective is to balance these ingredients in your personality. When they are balanced, out of such balance, they can just perform like a YOGI. So you can be a CEO Yogi in jeans and suit. You do not have to go to Himalayas by leaving all. When you act in balance, then your decisions and actions would be perfect as per the laws of Nature and then, the Nature, its unlimited energy will greatly support you and your incorporation. That is the aim of this book, which is the reason why, CEOs are called Arjuna in this book. Arjuna is a monk warrior who does the job of God for the welfare of the Nature. He did that job, to bring balance in the ingredients or traits of Nature. He did that with the guidance of Krishna the super natural power who was his driver, guide, preceptor, friend, guru, father and all.

Nature does not want you to leave your companies, families and take up monkhood. Nature does not want you to leave your sexual life or anything. Nature just wants all of those ingredients in balance. Only by keeping them in balance, you not only greatly help yourself, your family, your incorporation but also the whole cosmos and Nature. When they are in balance, the whole energy of

Nature would be there with you. It is called equilibrium level of personality. When all the traits act in balance, the material infrastructure of the world will prosper. If it prospers, obviously, your business, your money, your health, your happiness and all will flourish.

For example, let us take the element or the ingredient or trait, jealousy. When it is there in its balance level, you feel jealousy of others who are doing well or who are well off, then you work hard to reach that position. It will help you to fulfill your desires. After fulfilling the desire, you will not feel jealousy again in the same case as you already achieved it. You may get jealousy in some other case or desire. After achieving success in life, later, may be you feel jealousy of a politician, as you may want to become politician. So jealousy changes its forms positively.

So, in this case, the jealousy trait was positively helpful to you in your advancement. When the desires are fulfilled the thirst of the soul is achieved and then your feel happy which is what Nature wants. The same element jealousy can cross its limits, when it is applied negatively. Then it can even go to an extent of harming others and to commit some serious mistakes like crime and all.

Every trait is like a knife. If it is used well in its limitations, then it will help you to transform, achieve your desires and succeed. If it crosses its limits, then it gets negative and goes to an extent of doing negative actions in the world. Negative actions do not necessarily be crime, even if you hurt someone out of jealousy is an act of imbalance of it and such act earns you karma in the field of Nature. There may not be police for such small mistake of yours in the physical world but the police in Nature work always to register your imbalanced actions and to fine you which will reap you the karma.

In terms of Yogis, the total trait is killed, so they don't have any desires and they don't want to achieve anything. Yogi also works by consciousness and his consciousness helps the doers do their good works in the world. That way Yogis also work indirectly. But if everyone becomes Yogi, the show of the world does not run. Just like in your organization, there are thinkers, there are execution teams and there are doers. In the same way, the cosmic management works with all pools of consciousness.

So Nature wants you to be a Monk CEO who is in balance of all these but not Monk alone or CEO alone, but the combination of both that makes you a KARMA YOGI, who does actions out of harmony.

There are a couple of Sanskrit words called "Kshetra" and "Kshetrajna". Ksetra means, the field. Kshetrajna means, the one who is aware of the field. They both are used together to convey the message that you should be aware of your field well and that is when you can function well. If you are the CEO of a business, obviously you get to know many things about your industry and that is when you can function well. In the same way, you can function well, if you are aware of this field called "Nature" the Matrix of the world and that is when you can function well in business and all aspects of your life like Neil Anderson, Neo.

Nature also means externally five elements and the same five elements internally connect you with your five data input sense organs (mouth, ears, nose, skin, eyes) and the five output action points of the body. Nature also contains all those ingredients of traits as said above.

So Nature is there inside you and also it is there outside of you in the world. Nature is a field of energy in which various living beings, non-living beings and all are there. In the external world what do you get to see? You see, various other people, animals, plants and all and later if you further go, you get to see Sun, Moon, Five Elements and planets. But all these things exist in a field of time and space. That field is not a dead field and it is like an electro-magnetic field that works behind all these things that you see in the world.

From the cosmic sense, that field works like a host which is actually responsible to give required basic necessary things for its inhabitants.

In an imaginary way you can visualize Nature like a Mother's womb. That womb is the host of all living beings and non-living beings. Its ultimate aim is to sustain all the souls in it so that they can perform doing their karma.

No person in the world sits idle and even if he sits, his mind is restless. So in technical sense, every living being is active. Mind is quite active, pulsating emitting certain energies and generating its vibes with emotions all times.

The womb of Nature is required to give some basic infrastructure for the souls, so that they can live in it, sustain and burn their karma while living their lives.

The objective of the cosmic incorporation is to let all its employees and shareholders to know the environment of the company well, reach the CEO and finally unite with him, the owner of the cosmos whose form is pure universal consciousness.

In terms of the company in the real world, the CEO would have the body and he is a person. But in terms of the cosmic CEO, there is no person; it is the supreme consciousness that exists everywhere and all times without any beginning and ending. Some employees or some partners of the company would be able to reach CEO, only when they have transformed mind isn't it? Meaning, if you are the CEO, you would not simply allow any man to interact with you. Even if you allow, the system of your incorporation does not allow anyone to interact with you so easily. So whoever interacts with you, the CEO, needs to be transformed in terms of mind primarily and then the body would also need to have various other skills, discipline and good behavior in required frequency with the CEO.

That required frequency in a subtle way is nothing "like mindedness about your business and company". CEO's consciousness is expanded across the incorporation. He only meets people and interacts with people, who are in the process of getting such expanded consciousness in the company. Whoever expands their consciousness in the company, only those employees will transform and climb the hierarchy of the corporate ladder. Whose ever consciousness is expanded, they transform more like leaders and they do not remain like managers.

If you are given promotion it means, you are transformed and you have little expanded consciousness in the company which is the actual reason behind your promotion. You got promotion means, you have more earnings, more respect in the society and also in the firm. It is all prosperity isn't it? So what does the expansion of consciousness gets you ultimately? It is prosperity isn't it?

So the point I want to convey to you is – expansion of the consciousness that makes you selfless and make you more and more transformed in terms of personality which has direct impact on your work. Most of the people say, "What I have done is professional, not personal" - It means, that a person as professional, related to the work, he does his duty without any personal feelings, weaknesses attached. That means, that person acted in a way that is good for his for his duty or work and company. So he gave importance to his work and the company rather than himself and the others.

Company is the expanded field and he gave importance to that universal field of the company. Those kinds of actions are transformed actions that are good for the company and also for his personality.

Same kind of actions man has to do in the whole life, while living in this environment of the womb of Nature. Such selfless actions burn the karma of souls and then the souls transform and get out of the womb of Nature. You can check the picture below to have some understanding.

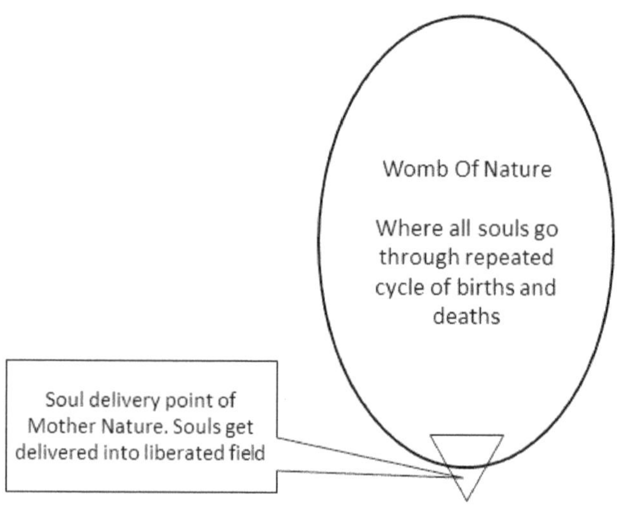

Thought the main objective of the creation is to liberate as many souls as possible from the womb of Nature, its immediate objective is to balance the ingredients of the souls in it so that the womb can remain in harmony. It wants to liberate most because, it cannot keep on bearing the weight of souls in it. Even disharmony in its womb, makes it have unbearable burning sensation in its stomach.

Both objectives i.e. liberation and harmony are possible only when the souls, burn their karmas that they owe to the field of Nature (this world) without accumulating new karmas. You work because you owe the karma to this world and your work adds value to the material infrastructure of the world. So your life is just a temporary stage in which you perform by working and burning your karma. But the problem is, you accumulate more karma while doing your already obligated karma. So the cycles of births and deaths increase more than the expected number, because of this. That increment of lives and births is a PAIN for the womb of Nature. Because, to those many number of souls, Nature has to give infrastructure and take care of them in its womb.

The cosmic CEO also has a strategy to manage the whole womb in a balanced way. But the souls, especially humans, because of the WILL they have, they carry more and more desires and their actions would always go against the laws of the womb and its objectives. Imagine, in your company, employees working against the laws of company and going away from the objectives of the company. If that is the case, your company can grow? You as a CEO, can you manage it and what actions will you take to bring back balance, so that the company can run well.

Do not say, so smartly that I don't care about this womb of Nature which I am not able to see and feel it. Well, you **do not have** to work and make your objective to be "getting liberated from the womb of Nature". That journey is quite profound and it is a very high end game, path and discipline and that path is of Yogis. It was already explained above in this chapter that Nature wants you to be a Monk CEO neither to be monk alone nor to be a CEO alone! It wants you to be a Karma Yogi, who acts in harmony with the laws of Nature, so that your business prospers, your society prospers and so does your country and the world.

But you will fall in the path of that main objective of the creation, if you learn to be in harmony with the womb and its environment or field. Simply to say, you should understand the wind flow, so you can work intelligently in harmony with the wind flow. Then, your life, your business, your way of dealing with people, all would get easier. Another advantage is that, as you have the energy of the wind with you, your flying gets effortless. If you are smart, you would try to understand this wind flow direction of the womb of Nature so that your journey of physical existence in the womb of Nature gets effortless, happy, peaceful and prosperous.

It is like you go to a country or city, after doing some research about that country or city in terms of its weather, its laws, people, economy and many more other things. Only then, you will visit that city or country. So you basically try to understand the field of the country and then you enter into its field.

So you are required to understand this field of womb of Nature, if you have to live by taking the help of the womb. Else, the life, the businesses and all become so laborious with drained efforts.

Another point you should remember is, this field of womb has enormous energies that are meant to be used by its inhabitants for their better living in its field. But still the humanity is taking only less than 5% of Nature's help. If that help increases, how fast and prosperous man can be while living in this womb.

There is a mechanism and algorithm by which this womb of Nature and its environment works. If that is known, man can benefit from its enormous energies. He can get lot of help and directions from the womb.

Listen to this carefully, while you read it, it will slip away easily from your mind – The journey of understanding this algorithm of Nature is quite long. But imagine, that is just available like a software program that can be installed in your system and imagine that software helps you understand the function of the Nature easily!

It is available in the format of a "software program" that can be just loaded into you.

This book at the end, leads you to such ways of "loading soul software programs of cosmic CEO" into you.

Chapter-9

The Field of Womb

You were presented the womb perspectives of the Nature in the previous chapter. If you understand the science of this womb and its field, then you and your business can get benefits in this field. You can evolve in harmony with the objectives of the womb and get immense strength from this field to prosper. In this chapter, you will understand the subtle, unseen and great works of Nature for the survival of its inhabitants.

Just like a tree, the womb is ultimately responsible to bear all its fruits and support them in order to ripen. All souls i.e. all living beings are hanging on to that tree of the cosmos trying to ripen.

The womb is like a tree that keeps working in an unseen and subtle way which can only be perceived by the inner eye.

Womb works mainly with the wheel of time and space. It has its own laws that cannot be documented. All souls when they touch their innate Nature they can know all its laws and work in harmony with its laws. The problem comes when they don't touch their innate Nature and it is quite difficult for the man at this juncture of time and space. That is when man looks for external help of books or internet to know how to act when. So he pays some money and adopts various meditational techniques etc. But all of them only can get little temporary peace except which nothing more he gets. He does that meditation, out of lot of efforts. So technically no one really feels like doing meditation. So, people just meditate for few minutes or maximum couple of hours who are experts at it. But imagine, if meditation happens all times without your efforts!

Coming back to our main thread about Nature, you know very well that even if you go to amazon forest, if you see a man, you do not hit him or kill him right? Because your inner Nature tells you that it is wrong to do so. So the awakening is all about touching that INNATE NATURE OF YOUR TRUE SELF that knows everything. No one has to teach your inner Nature nor has anyone to guide you. But you are required to be given the method of touching it, and then you will know it yourself!

The womb of Nature, has unlimited energies using which it operates. It energizes mainly the five elements which are the gross source of every physical thing or material in the world. Using those energies, we are able to build and make several physical material objects. Roads, buildings, cars, mobiles all physical things are made of these primary energy sources of five elements. Not just those objects, the subtle energies behind our senses are also of five elements. So without five elements, man cannot survive. I am sure you know what the five elements are – earth, water, fire, air and space.

The world or the womb of Nature is actually a field of Five Elements and their play in its time and space. The people who are living in this world, they meet various people, they work, they interact with various people and live their lives. Everybody is actually a soul, from the perspectives of the womb of Nature and the souls evolve through various bodies in it by taking various births and deaths. For every living being, the womb has to provide required infrastructure which are like five elements and secondly the energy of Nature has to work behind these souls LIKE A PUSH mechanism behind their minds that actually make them to take several actions and also meet various other souls.

Imagine someone is looking for a job and he tries to apply for various jobs and he keeps putting efforts in getting the job he wants. He, as a soul, has his own energies, desires, intentions and WILL to work on his own. But behind him, the field that he is living in is also working with him in a subtle way, in order to meet him with his objectives of life. For the field, evolution of the soul is more important. The soul may evolve through various bodies, but through every birth it carries its own karmas that it owes to the womb or the world. The obligated karmas have to be paid back by the souls and the world. The bodies may not remember because of their mind limitations. But their souls in the background work in collaboration with the field of MATRIX, The Nature to meet their objectives in every life.

The objectives of every soul in every life are recorded in the field of Nature or womb or Matrix. Your soul naturally triggers the Nature to live in its field for which the unlimited energy of Nature cooperates and works like a push mechanism in the background of your body and soul which you cannot perceive by your mind.

Imagine you are looking for some job or business opportunities and you approach various people. But some of them come back to you and with some of them only you do the business, actually. There is an unknown push mechanism that is working behind you and the people whom you meet. The backgrounds of those people, their souls interact with the field of Nature based on various permutations and combinations of algorithm of Nature and then they come forward to interact with you.

The objectives of Nature and its field are only to connect you to the other souls whom you actually owe your karma. But you have your own mind and WILL, out of which you develop some preferences and then you choose only certain people or opportunities to work with. Those preferences may kill the karma that you already owe to the womb of Nature (in case you naturally or coincidentally or luckily choose those people to whom you owe your karma) or you may develop new karma without killing the old baggage of karma, if you open new interaction again with new people.

The souls or the inhabitants of the womb of Nature are actually living their lives in a dream state. They do not actually wake up for several lives together. The dream state of theirs is so illusionary that they run after those false illusions for several lives together. You only study in schools and colleges may be for 15 to 18 years. But after completion of various levels of education, you would take up some profession and work. When you studied in schools and colleges, your parents must have funded your education and your living. But imagine, you want to study for many years like 30 or 40 years. Will they be able to fund you all these years for your education and living? Imagine, you forcibly live like that with your parents. Because of their love towards you, parents may bear you for few years, but definitely one day, it becomes a complete unbearable situation for them. In the same way, for this WOMB of Nature, the souls are living in a dream state like this, as lifelong students who want to depend forever on parents. The parents keep trying their best level to wake up this sleeping child who is a big weight for them. In the same way, the womb keeps trying its best to wake up its dreaming children from their dreams. But due to the accumulation of new karmas, they again and again get into new dreams for thousands of lives together.

The womb is also a great infrastructural field which is flourishing with great efforts as all its inhabitants keep on working for it and also towards it. Just go back to thirty years. We did not have mobile phones. We did not have several other comforts such as internet etc. But today, this world which is a field of womb of Nature in which we are living is so well developed and it keeps on flourishing more and more which is an endless process. The souls work for some years and their bodies die and they again take up new bodies, get born in the same womb of Nature and again they keep working like burning their souls. Actually they feel like burning because they actually work towards burning their dreams (which are karmas) and results of their karmas add value to this whole infrastructure of the womb. But how long this show of dreams of souls goes on? There is a life span for the womb from the creation perspectives.

The womb has a self-sustaining system that again gains energies from its own inhabitants. Just like a crop, yielding from the field, imagine you keep putting more and more seeds in the same field without fertilizing the field, the yield of every crop would get lesser and lesser for every cycle of the crop. In the same way, the yield of this womb also gets reduced if the crop of souls in the womb does not mature at the expected rate. The expected rate of evolution or transformation of souls is not known to souls but the womb knows.

If you understand the womb of Nature, its objectives and its subtle operations of time and space of souls, you will be able to properly work in harmony with the womb. Such harmony, though, it does not speed up the womb's evolution, but it definitely adds value like a bearable pain to the womb.

You can understand how Nature and its responsible moving energy, meets the souls as per their needs, by seeing the street dogs and other animals or birds. The street dogs and animals do not have any professions like you to earn money and eat food. They just get hinted in their minds about the availability of the food. The same energy of Nature also makes some people to think of waste food and then they give it to street dogs. It is all the work of moving energy of Nature that does all these subtle operations. If you miss the hint of the Nature, then it will hint somebody else, in your street to give the food to the dogs. The same operation happens in all animals and birds. Now you will understand who is the actual doer? It is that moving energy of Nature which is the actual doer of all the things. It is the darkness of the bodies that make them think that they are the doers.

When it comes to your business, you will find same kind of operations of Nature in the background. In terms of business, especially in sales, there is a high involvement of Nature and its energy. The business man or the corporation makes its products with the vision and intention of good energy that its products should help many people in the world. Nature and its moving energy in the background, collects those visions, emotions and intentions from the consciousness levels of all souls, who work in that company. Then, it will match your products with the people who need your products in the consciousness level. This operation happens in the consciousness level, which is a deep layer of all souls.

The whole world and the entire womb of Nature is an integrated field of consciousness. It is like for example, a magnetic field. In that field, imagine, all living beings live. Though everyone has their own minds and wills, there is a subtle background work of magnetic field in which all bodies live. That magnetic field is responsible to run the show of the world or womb of Nature and thus it does all subtle works. One of those works of Nature is "meeting your needs with some others who need your needs". It is the main operation of every business. Just like the way how a match making software automatically does the match making based on various permutations and combinations, in the same way, Nature and its integrated consciousness meets the souls based on various permutations and combinations of karma, traits, and their personal or universal emotions and so on.

If you know how software works, what I am saying here would help you understand quickly. The business man's visions, intentions, feelings his needs are collected in data format by the Nature. Then, that data is stored in a mega memory of the Nature and its consciousness (which is an integrated consciousness). Then, into the same consciousness of Nature, the data of people who need such products also will get stored. Then a kind of business analysis work or match making work is done by an algorithm of Nature.

Then that algorithm matches the needs of "supply" and "demand" in the integrated consciousness. Then, after such work, the energy of Nature hints their needs (of both supply and demand souls). Remember, the work of Nature is only to HINT all the souls (of demand and supply) in their minds. The HINTS appear in the form of images, sound and thought formats in the mind. It is a very subtle operation of Nature. Only people who are into high end of spiritual practices who study their minds and mind movements, they get to see these visions with their awareness. Meaning, their awareness gets so sharp based on their spiritual practices so that they can scan the images, the sound formats and thoughts that are appearing in their minds. Based on their WILL, they will again act upon such visions and hints of Nature.

But in terms of normal people like you, the same images appear which are like hints for you to act upon them. But your awareness is not sharp and your mind is also so chaotic with too many visions, pictures and sounds and soul talks within. Your minds are full of many matters and subjects in the world. So your mind is not that sharp to recognize those hints of Nature. However, even if the normal man's awareness is dull, out of many of such Nature's hints, he can at least collect few hints and act upon them. This is called intuition and some people who have good awareness, will have strong feeling to follow those directions and act upon them. Even those people do not know that, it is actually subtle operation of Nature. They only think that somehow they are lucky to have such skill and sharp mind. But it is actually a subtle operation of Nature that works in all living beings equally.

Some people have sharp awareness and some do not have such awareness.

This is how; the sellers and buyers are met by Nature. Now you may ask, Why Nature is doing all this work? Nature does not have any work or what? – The point is NATURE is THE WOMB in which all are living. It works like a HOST and it is ultimately responsible more than your parents and all, to give a platform for your soul to live, so that your body sustains and if your body sustains, then its soul will evolve. If its soul evolves, its karma will add value to the infrastructure of the womb, then the soul's karma will be burnt then, the soul has high possibility of ripening like a fruit and transforming so that it can get out of the cage of Nature's womb which is called the freedom to the soul. Getting FREEDOM to a soul will lessen the burden of the womb of Nature. Even if it does not get freedom, in that process, the soul at least gets in harmony which is a great value addition to the cosmic womb. This is the ultimate objective and responsibility of the Nature. As part of its work, it does its operations in terms of sustaining the bodies in her womb.

As part of that work, sustaining the bodies of the souls is the primary step. In the first step, it actually addresses "professions, work, earnings" of people. The work and professions burn the karmas of souls. Then earnings help them get money so that they can eat food and meet their comforts in life. Comforts in life are the secondary objective for the Nature.

The secondary objective of Nature is the primary objective for men as they are selfish.

Did you ever observe sometimes, when you go visit some markets, you find several shops into same businesses in a street. Sometimes you will find hundreds of shops being into the same business and selling the same products. But isn't it so strange that all of them survive. You can get same kind of product from every shop. Despite heavy competition, they all survive. It is purely because of the Nature's unseen work that happens in the background.

If you observe movie business, movie makers, make movies and sell to distributors and they further advertise on TVs and other media channels etc. But how many people really get to see those advertisements and how many people actually go to theatres and buy tickets to watch that movie? Behind it there is a very subtle operation of Nature. The same operation of Nature happens with every product and service available in the world.

Nature only helps those people who have good intentions. Nature does not hint people who have bad intentions. Do not say that, a bad man doing some crime has hints of Nature. Nature does not hint minds who carry bad intentions. It is their own mind and their own consciousness that works and then they do those bad actions.

So right from a big international corporation to a small business like a carpenter, all are able to survive in this womb of Nature because of the involvement of Nature and its energy in the background. Of course, their own mind, their skill, smartness, will, desire, good intentions and all definitely play some role from their ends. Rest of the operation is a cosmic operation that happens in the background as explained so far. That operation works the same for all humans, except for those who have bad intentions. There is a sloka in Bhagawadgita, in which Krishna says - "Arjuna, just do your karma at your best and leave the results to me, do not worry about the results". He says that because, seabed of consciousness always works all that I said so far. If your work is honest and tried at all its best levels, the software of the cosmic CEO's consciousness does its best match making for you and helps you with the best results. Normal people, after reading that sloka, even some high end spiritualists do not know this background operation of the cosmic CEO's consciousness. That is what you get when you hire Krishna as your driver! You hire him? Or he hires you? – think!

So imagine, if you have the intelligence and interactive capability with Nature and its operations, how greatly it will add value to your business? It will definitely add value but you are required to be in harmony with its laws and have good intentions for the welfare of the people of the world. Then, that energy will work for you. That means, you are required to move a little to MONK SIDE, wearing the same suit of CEO. Little movements of such will greatly encourage you later to take big leaps that will greatly help you in personal life and also in terms of Business.

It requires some sacrifice, discipline, developing good habits, positive attitude and several other things. Do not think it's hard for you. If you take some initial steps, just like smoking habit, all that discipline will come into your life involuntarily. The Online Transformation School from Hariom Movement, will introduce you all those practices and disciplines which you can practice from home, if you are interested.

Chapter-10

Time And Space And Its Evolution

World is the play of matrix of time, space and mind i.e. your lower self. It is the evolution of time and space tied to your evolution.

It is one of the works of Nature. Nature works with you by time and space. Of course you carry your own will, desires, preferences based on which at times you lag behind and at times you advance, in terms of chronology of situations. Based on the desires and preferences most of the times, you are not able to meet the moving frequency of Nature at its pace of time and space. In order to recognize its hints and movements and actions of people in the external world requires, subtle mind. To get subtle mind, primarily you need to have good intentions and then with the effort of some discipline and simple practices you can get it.

Nature works with you, your time and karma and accordingly it connects you to several other souls and situations in day to day life. Your true self or the higher self does not move but your mind only moves in the matrix of time and space. Your true self has to transform from lower self to its true self in the travel movement.

The evolution wheel of time and space of Nature moves on irrespective of your evolution. But do you have the capability of tuning to its frequency so that you can move with its evolution? Are you in harmony with its frequency so you can evolve involuntarily?

If you get in harmony with its frequency, all its unlimited energies would come to you to evolve you. Your evolution in terms of soul and prosperity in life, they are directly connected to the movement of Nature's time and space. This movement of Nature's wheel has got immense power behind it and it moves on its own irrespective of anyone participating in its movement. But if you could join its movement, you will be able to move involuntarily without much effort. This book will connect you finally to such involuntary evolution. If you could join its movement, your life, your business, finances, health, all would move with the wheel of Nature, involuntarily.

In terms of businesses, you know pretty well that the way businesses were run and the way they used to evolve was quite slower in the old days. Old does not mean, many decades ago. If you just go back to 80s and 90s, the way the businesses were run was totally slow paced and then the time and space did not need fast minds of today. Minds also require evolution based on Nature and its atmospheric evolution, mainly connected with technology. If you are a CEO, you cannot definitely operate your business the way you used to operate way back in 80s and 90s. It works the same right from CEO level to even lower level executives in the incorporation. If you are in late forties or early fifties by age, if you look back the way you started your career and if you compare yourself with the new comers, I am sure, you agree that, you were quite behind in terms of their way of thinking, their skills, their natural talent etc.

I am sure you find them more multi skilled and extra talented and extra informative unlike you were in your old days. That itself is the evolution you are able to see in front of your eyes. This is the human mind and its evolution in just couple of decades which happened due to the evolution of the time and space of the external world and it has its own impact of evolution on the internal minds and lives of today's people. Obviously the kind of skills, talent required in their professions became day to day activities in their lives. Today, even a man who does not pass out high school is able to do pretty well in technologies and their usage. Even a man who is well educated, in mid-fifties is not able to catch up with the technology usage. That is the evolution of internal world of the human connected with the evolution of the external world.

All these I had to say, to present you that "the evolution" of the time and space goes on and it is not in your hands. You are required to evolve with it. You evolve, you are in the game, you do not evolve, you are out of the game!

In the same lines, if you compare the openness of the human mind today in terms of relationships and dealing with people is more evolved unlike the old days.

The way of operating businesses, the way you deal with your employees and other partners is totally different today unlike old days. You do not much see subordination in business relationships today. That becomes a weakness if it is carried in today's way of operating business. If businesses are operated that way, it will become a major hurdle for them. That attitude is not carried by today's business operators' generation. You may be a king but today's world is so smart that even the king has to smartly deal with the people and relations, else he will be out of his game. That itself is the example that you see in today's businesses.

So the point is about evolution of your mind in terms of its expansion.

Keeping others low to you, being authoritative towards others, applying your political mind to suppress others, covering your mistakes, supporting your mistakes and all such personality related weaknesses do not work for today's CEO. In next couple of decades, the business environments are going to demand more openness from both CEOs, top executives and also from other employees down below.

If you see the man and his evolution, from a man of forest, man became a well cultured man, living in the society. He evolved with the time and space.

Do not think, it is man who evolved the world. The point again comes to the PUSH force of Nature that actually applies on human minds which is actually the doer. That doing act of Nature is what is today's infrastructure and technology. It is push energy of the wheel of time and space of Nature that actually runs the world by moving even mountains and oceans. The wheel of Nature moves on as per its evolution by pushing all to its required pace.

The technology of software came into existence to show the reality of mind and its contents to the world. It is the work of Nature. Nature purposely evolves the world and its infrastructure to teach the souls to expand their consciousness which happens by giving up their weaknesses.

I am talking about the world being at the edge of taking the humanity into NEXT LEVEL EVOLUTION OF HIS MIND and CONSCIOUSNESS. But are you ready to catch up the speed of Nature and its evolution? You are required to catch up else, how educated ever you are, how smart ever you are, you cannot meet its frequency and you get outdated. The whole atmosphere of the Nature and its algorithm would change and in that field, you and your business cannot sustain when you are not updated.

The material world always moves towards more and more subtle side of it. Meaning though it has physicality, it would have its own virtual aspects introduced to the world. That is the result of software, information technology, internet, smart phones, VR sets, IOTs and all. That change was forcibly brought by the cosmic CEO who took the new charges in late seventies!

Today, even a common man is using smart phone widely and even if he is not educated, he knows all the operations of it. Virtuality is nothing but mind and the surfing of it. Most of the people today are lost into that virtual world. Without even knowing time, many people for nothing they keep browsing through their phones. That is actually a Nature's push of humans to get into virtuality because, that is how, they can kill their negative energies and also their minds will get more subtler and along with that, several humans watch the same content and spend more time with that content with their emotions and feelings behind which they are actually touching the integrated consciousness of the seabed. Unlike TV, the content on smart phones is felt more by all subtle side organs of human systems.

The new management given to Kalki, the latest cosmic energy version of the super natural power, the latest version of the cosmic CEO, in order to bring transformation in human consciousness, he introduced this sift in the worldly things and the shift is all about virtuality that will make humans more and more subtler to start their inward journey.

In a way, unlike spiritual ashrams and Gurus, the unseen work of the cosmic CEO would come like a huge wave of change that pushes the world in certain direction that brings transformation in them involuntarily without even talking or preaching!

The virtual shift of the physical world, would make the man more and more subtler which will help the human consciousness as a whole to transform.

That transformation of the world towards virtuality and virtuality related things would also demand the transformation of humans who work in those areas who produce them and also in those humans who use those products and services. Meaning, their minds, their way of thinking, their way of working, their way of interacting with people, transparency in their working cultures, their way of management and many more would naturally fall in harmony, as the environments of Nature, naturally would demand them.

This is how, the cosmic CEO, if he wants change; one wave of this kind could bring transformation in human consciousness quite faster in a revolutionary way, without setting up and yoga studios and ashrams that teach yoga to the people. That change would be quite slow process, whereas this natural operation would forcibly push the whole humanity into its mode of operations and directions.

This shift in human consciousness came from late seventies that brought the evolution in electronics field that further pushed itself into computers, from there it went to internet and then to smart phones and then to VR and IOTs and all.

It will further more push the world towards virtuality to get the humans more and more subtler, softer and kinder and at the same time, whatever the negativity they earn in the physical world, they would burn out all of it in this virtual world by killing their time and energies unknowingly! There is a big cosmic strategy behind all these shifts in order of worldly things.

The cosmic CEO who took the charges by late 70s, brought all this transformation in the human consciousness and he is Kalki, the tenth incarnation of lord Vshnu. You will be given couple of mantras in later chapters by which you will be able to tune to his frequency and get guided by him just like the way Krishna helped Arjuna. He is the current cosmic CEO who has taken the management charges. You do not believe it as you read all these, but you experience with the formulas given in the later chapters.

So the bottom line is, this shift in the world by cosmic operation is to bring harmony in human consciousness so that humans could think, act and function in harmony with the laws of Nature. It is going to be a cosmic operation of few thousands of years. Without any physical wars, discussions and preaches, human consciousness will naturally get harmony and there will be several operations as such will be initiated in the Nature by that cosmic CEO, Hare Kalki.

This is all his work of time and space in Nature.

The update first is required in the mind, not in terms of material updates! The evolution is always about going forward to more and more of expansion of yourself. Your business also always aims at more and more expansion. Prior to material business and its expansion, it is the consciousness of the business that has to expand in the CEO's mind, then in that consciousness of his, the expanded-business will exist. The expansion comes by getting more and more perfect in terms of personality which falls more and more in harmony with the laws of Nature.

Words such as openness, welcoming new things, new people, new thoughts, new talents, new skills, applauding them, moving with them, accepting failure boldly, sacrificing the personal ego for the welfare of THE ENTIRITY, all these are high end qualities of leadership and Arjuna, which will be highly demanded to stay in the game of today's world and tomorrow's world would demand much higher degree of these things.

Every man is getting smarter day by day, his mind is expanding and his consciousness is expanding the sourcecode of man is getting more and more open and thus all humans would get more and more open which requires openness of personality by hugging universality.

So, are you ready to evolve or you say you are old man, an old executive and you want to do your business and live personal life in that shrunk consciousness or will you kill your ego and do business with younger generations, by expanding your consciousness?

To stay ahead of the tomorrow's generation, you need to know the art of expanding your consciousness and that's the only way, you as a CEO can evolve and stay ahead with tomorrow's world. Else, you will be left alone behind! Imagine the treadmill is moving at its set speed, if you can't catch up its speed, you will be thrown out.

So are you ready to expand or shrink? To expand your consciousness, you do not have to go to moon or Himalayas! You can get it right there where you are. The expansion of consciousness includes elements such as "managing mind space, browsing the mindspace, vibes and their energies".

So the question is – how many times did you think about "so and so thing of your business today"? Do not say simply, so many times vaguely!

What is the frequency of thoughts that you had in your mind space today?

Can you catch up the speed of your mind and its high speed navigation of thoughts? What is the way?

If this art is known, your consciousness will expand across your business through cellular levels of it!

Evolution is the only way that is left for human. He is thrown into the world of treadmill and it has its own speed that keeps changing as per Nature's evolution. Catch up its speed or you are thrown out! It does not require you to worry and pressurize yourself to get it. It is not something you get it. It is there within you and it has to awaken and shine and its process is a subtle one!

You may be running a business that has few branches around the world or your country, but do you have your consciousness expanded to all those branches? If so, you would know every moment the major happenings in those branches by mind without physical updates via emails or text messages but just knowing by mind.

Knowing by information is worldly way of knowing but knowing by consciousness is a next level thing! Doing actions by consciousness (not physical actions) is much higher level of it and it can happen with CEOs who become Arjunas. Do you browse or navigate your business by your consciousness?

Do not get misguided by thinking that, just thinking about your business itself means consciousness. No, you have not yet experienced the consciousness. You will experience it, when the cosmic CEO comes forward and gives you an air lift! Consciousness is an ocean which you cannot swim but imagine, you swim on the shoulders of the cosmic CEO and go through the ocean. Then, you can effortlessly surf the ocean and then you will know that you are not body but something else and to know that you do not have to take up any monkhood! But just by becoming the Monk CEO, you can do so!

Chapter-11

CEO And Karma

Karma is basically the "work" that you owe to the world. Karma in a way also means "action" that you do. Through several births and deaths you have been logging into the same womb of Mother Nature as you basically carry your own desires that actually get fulfilled by your actions.

But the problem is, you do not know how to do the actions in the atmosphere of the womb. Because you do not know how the womb functions i.e. how the Nature functions. So, in the process of fulfilling your desires, you again get trapped in new karmas that you have to pay back to the Nature or the world. So, some of the karmas that you owe to the world, you may not like them. Karmas such as you hit someone, you cheat someone, you mock at someone, you harm someone and so on earn you back the pains which you will not like to bear. In the process of fulfilling your desires, you tend to do these actions in the world which accumulate your karma which has to be paid back to the cosmos. The results of these actions come back to you in the form of bad health, financial issues, relationship issues, being under the control of others and so on. You do not like these results that come from the cosmic womb because they cause you pain. But everyone is required to pay back their karma as per the algorithm of the Nature and its laws which no one can escape.

So, the bottom line is you do some job, you do some business and you do something in the world because of either your desires or because of the payback that you have to do to the cosmic womb. So the point is, you need to work, you need to act. From the Cosmic Womb perspectives, what should be purpose of your actions?

Your actions should ultimately give you soul satisfaction and every action of yours should have some impact in the "progress" of the world. Your actions should expand your consciousness. So you should question yourself, if your actions actually help the world to progress or they hinder the progress of the world or its inhabitants. You need to question like that because you are not a normal human, you are the CEO of a corporation who is actually doing a cosmic job. You should achieve this by not committing any of those mistakes that are against the laws of Nature such as cheating others, hurting others, harming others and so on. Actions do not mean just physical actions, such thoughts also would produce their own related karma.

When you do actions that expand your consciousness then your mind and intellect get cleansed. While the old karmas get cleared, the new karmas should stop their accumulation which is the art of Karma Yogi which you will know. As the karma clears, you will also evolve well in terms of your material life.

Did you ever think that you work hard but the results are not up to the mark? It is because of purely the old baggage of karma that you carry on your head in an unseen way. There are various methods to get rid of such loads and then you can start getting tangible results in your business and personal life.

This point is very important for a CEO because, his actions would impact on the progress of the incorporation. His incorporation is not a simple separated entity from the cosmic womb or the world or Nature. The CEO's incorporation itself is a small cosmos by it, which is connected with the holistic Nature in which all exist. As said earlier as the companies play the vital role in the evolution of Nature, CEO's actions would have their own impact on the business and life span of the company. His decisions should be as per the laws of Nature or the cosmic womb. Situationally everybody does mistakes, in businesses. Those mistakes might appear to be small and that may TEMPORARILY fix the problems but again and again, over again the same situations occur in your business to see you transform.

When you transform, you would become impersonal personal. But irrespective of transformation, the actions done would reap their results for the company.

CEO is not just an executive who mastered his education in some business school. CEO literally means a KING of a kingdom. A king is supposed to have an impersonal personality which means a universal personality. A true king actually sacrifices his personal life for the welfare of the people and others.

A king has to see all his people including his family members as children. If you check the history, you can count such kind of kings in fingers. World hardly had such kings. There was a king in India, who was called "Janak" the father of Sita. He used to be such king. He was called "The Monk King".

So is the CEO. A CEO becomes Monk when he functions in harmony with the laws of Nature or the Cosmic Womb by knowing his importance in the evolution of The Nature and he becomes Arjuna, the best Karma Yogi.

As a CEO you need to have a universal personality. You not only act impersonal in terms of your own business but externally as well, with all other business relations in the world. You need to have such universal personality.

Because of competition and several other situations in the business, most of the CEOs act with their limited personalities which are against the laws of Nature. The actions of such CEOs may temporarily help the incorporation but, on the long life of the incorporation such actions would have greater impact that could challenge the existence of the incorporation.

False promises to people, favoring some friends or close relations, harming others who grow by their talent, harming other businesses or competition, expecting commissions at the pain of others, paying low or unjustifiably etc. are some of the actions of CEOs that are against the laws of Nature. Such actions not only harm the incorporation but also the personal life of such CEOs. Though some CEOs are disciplined in this kind of actions, some would have illusion.

Illusion comes out desires of fame, recognition, financial gain and other gains. Actions that are aimed towards such personal importance would most of the times fail. Even if few times, they succeed, those results are a BIG TRAP for big loss stored in the future.

Business schools do not teach the education related to cosmic womb and its laws. In fact the laws of Nature and how to act when cannot be recorded in books. Even few million books of such situations would fall short for the humans to follow the laws of Nature.

Following laws of Nature is called a system of “DHARMA”. Dharma is a system by itself. Even great sages and monks in the history of human race could not perfectly follow THE DHARMA. Understanding DHARMA is difficult but “how to act when” has to be loaded into you like a software.

Just like the way, when you drive a car, how you act spontaneously in a specific situation, to avoid the accident? You cannot learn it by reading books. In the same way, you cannot know as to how to act in a specific situation in life by reading books. Did anyone teach you how to act in a specific situation that may arise on the road, in driving car? Or you read any book and learnt? It cannot be learnt by reading books or by listening to some holy speeches of a monk!

So far in the world, they practiced certain yogic methods, to learn Dharma. But man has lost all his energies to follow those yogic methods. Man is not able to meet the basic discipline required for such practices. At the current point of time and space, man cannot learn Dharma by such practices and the negative energies are so powerful to invade him and again inject negativity into him. So there has to be some new technology that should transform man involuntarily to know the Dharma and also protect him further so that the negativity does not slip into him again.

Imagine the discipline and the dharma loading into you like software with its energy. In fact the art of driving the car, you learn, based on the experience of driving many miles. You get to learn the art of driving a car, more and more as you drive more miles.

Just imagine there is a software that loads into you "the art of driving" which, also comes with energy of it. Then, it can make you act "as per the laws of

Nature" involuntarily in any situation that could come up randomly in life.

Obviously DHARMA is something that cannot be learnt by reading books or by listening to speeches of monks or great sages. Their speeches can only impress you, excite you, encourage you towards taking steps such steps in your life. Bad habits, weaknesses, personalities and actions are stored in your soul software which cannot be erased by listening to some lectures of a monk or reading books. They cannot even be erased even if you do thousands of hours of meditation.

You invest in taking up some personality development courses but the courses do not inject any spiritual energy in you.

If you are a smoker, you do not have energies that can overcome your bad habit. Nicotine has greater energy than you that supersedes your soul energy. Because of its higher energy, you are not able to quit smoking. Nicotine is controlling you and it has higher energy than your soul. You cannot quit smoking by taking any management course or personality development course.

Imagine there is an injection available that can empower your soul in terms of energy. Then, you can easily and effortlessly overcome your smoking habit. It is a medicine of spiritual energy that heals your soul on one side and also injects overcoming energies.

In the same way, there is a spiritual medication supplied by the cosmos, which you can tune to. It is a frequency of the cosmic CEO, to which you can tune to. Then you start getting such spiritual energies loaded into you gradually, but not at one shot! You improve as you the spiritual energy loads more into you. If your indiscipline increases, then the software also starts unloading automatically!

The super natural power as the cosmic CEO, has a great responsibility to make sure that the creation runs for few millions of years as per its plan of cycle. Several great challenges from the negative energies came in the history of the creation that challenged the existence of human race. But all times, the Cosmic CEO came out well with his own plans and his divine team of executives.

His incorporation is so huge and he, as a BIG CEO of the cosmos, is also responsible equally to help you, the worldly CEO to manage your business well. He will help you because your KARMA is also part of his KARMA. Cosmic CEO's karma is superset in which your karma is subset!

His KARMA is a selfless responsibility for the sustenance of the creation. Do not think, he owes something to the world. He does not owe anything. He can remain like consciousness without body, but he comes into the MUD of MANAGING the cosmos out of selfless love for the cosmos, which is his OWN SELF. Your incorporation is also a SELFLESS creation of yours (if you are the CEO who created your business) for which you selflessly work or have to work. After certain level of your business you as a CEO see it yourself as if it is more than just a business that gives you money for your benefits! You see it much bigger than that. You as a normal human and CEO can feel that after few years of starting your business. That means your consciousness out of your hard work expands and gets selfless more and more.

So, in a way, you as a CEO of your incorporation, if you tune to the cosmic CEO's frequency, you will start playing a role in the COSMOS MANAGEMENT indirectly. You are actually helping THE NATURE in balancing its cosmic womb. When you play that role, imagine the kind of immense energy, help and protection you get from the whole cosmos!

So the karma of yours as a CEO is also partially KARMA of the Cosmic CEO, whom the religions call God and he is the best Karma Yogi.

But you can call him simply out of love Cosmic CEO, the boss who is a true friend, father and so on, available to you just a THOUGHT AWAY at his frequency.

Chapter-12

CEO And Simplicity

When you know the truth, that you are on par with any animal or human on the earth, then irrespective of your financial status, talent or education etc. you would stay on grounds without any showoff.

Showoff comes out of your pride that differentiates you, from others. But the question is who others are? The so called others you are thinking of, are actually your own mirror images in this cosmic womb. If you showoff, it will come back to you. If you hurt someone, it will come back to you. If you cheat someone, it will come back to you. It will come back ten times more if you hurt someone. Just like a ball, if you throw it to the wall, it will come back to you much faster. In the same way, your every emotion, thought and action will come back to you in this field of mirror images of your own self. Having known this truth, whom will you show off now? Or is it that your trait that awakens from within when someone shows off to you, you do the same! You don't have to do it, because someone else did it. They do it out of weakness that they cannot control whereas you as the CEO, you are not weak;

you would have the cosmic energy with you by which you can still remain calm without any reactions to it.

Just because someone else does actions against the Nature, you don't have to follow them out of provocation.

So the point is, you are just any other being, living in this womb of Nature who is there to get rid of their karma that they owe to the cosmic womb. A beggar is there on the earth and so are you, so is dog and so is me. What difference do we all have in the actual sense? As you get rid of your karma, you will excel in your business, in your careers and in your personal lives.

Monkey when it knows some art or skill or some knowledge or something, it will always show off to others – saying, you see what "I know". So you will have to think yourself, if you want to be like that monkey or the one who can control the show off baggage. The baggage can vary from money to cars to talent to language to clothing to culture to religion and many other things.

Controlling this show off business is the first step towards simplicity. Another thing that has to be acquired is, if others showoff, you may not have to buy their showoff and at the same time, you do not have to frown on them. You can adopt the attitude of watching them rather. This showoff is an attitude that is carried by most of the people. This is the root cause that will build big ego and it further gets pumped to commit quite bigger mistakes in life. So controlling it will get a greater benefit in all aspects of life.

The bottom line is all about burning the karma that you owe to this cosmos. So do it carefully without further buying new karmas in their burning process. The point is that everyone in the womb of Nature, woes to it. From its perspectives, there is no difference and we do not have to build those non sensible differences based on various status levels in the society.

To live a simple life, accept the way the life is creating situations in the world. Situations come to burn your karmas. Nature creates those situations for you to evolve further. Some situations may temporarily appear to be painful. But when you go through them, the environment of the cosmic womb will also give you immense strength to overcome them. Going through those situations is like accepting the LAW of Nature. When you accept the situations irrespective of the people involved in the situations, you tend to kill your FALSE EGO. That false ego killing will expand your consciousness and get you immense happiness and strength. You tend to become more and more modest.

If the situations turn out to be like disgrace for you, accept the disgrace. You don’t have to show your physical muscle to tussle with the disgrace. People who watch you in disgrace and when you accept and remain silent that will in fact build immense sympathy and everyone will appreciate you. The one who disgraces you obviously would be in uncontrollable anger, frowning on you in various actions out of mouth. From the cosmic sense, they are out of control. That balanced way of your being is simplicity. Simplicity does not just mean, driving your own car, cleaning your own floor, though they are in a way, in their own lower sense. Practice of this, would help you big in your business.

Sometimes in business decisions, you are required to pull back and step back. If they are required, taking that step is much better than going for false egoistic moves that actually will hurt the business. That bending and pulling back is a kind of stamping your false ego. This kind of steps though, others may temporarily laugh at you, for your decisions, you can accept those disgraces and move on. Nature will have its own time built for you that will naturally show those laughed ones, what you are.

There is a guarantee given by the Nature that says – When you follow the Dharma, the Dharma itself protects you all times! Dharma itself is God. More than God, the name of the Truth is Dharma. Even in tough times, without committing mistakes against the laws of Nature, would always give you immense strength and Nature has something greater in her womb to give you back in the future for your sacrifice to stand by the Dharma.

How many times, you must have cooked your own food, even if you are a CEO of a big incorporation? Or how many times you should have washed your dishes and cleaned your bathrooms or drove your cars.

The point is, do not avoid the answer by saying that you are quite busy and your time is quite valuable. Man is required to do some basic required works that he is actually meant to do and he is answerable to the Nature. Such basic works actually connect to the KARMA BURNING process of yours that will awaken various ideas in the business problems you have.

While doing some of those works, great ideas and resolutions will flash in your mind naturally. Doing those basic works, in a way keep your ego at its level so it will not bounce unnecessarily and those works (karma) are indirectly connected to the karma in personal life or in business. Because of that connection, as the karma is burnt while doing those basic works, resolutions for certain problems will suddenly flash in your mind. That obligated karma is like a lock that holds from getting the resolutions for some problems in life and business. Not just ideas, there are some people connected to such karma you do. When you do those basic works, the people who are causing problems to you in your business or life, may cooperate with you by opening the lock. This is one of the algorithms on which Nature works. You can implement this in your life and check practically. It does not mean, playing tennis or golf or doing some physical exercises are like karma burning. They do not come under karma burning as per the laws of the Nature. Those actions are basically unproductive in terms of karma. Those actions do not help you in burning the karma that you owe to the cosmos.

How busy executive ever you are, certain basic functions of life need to be undergone to perfectly deal with the business life. Saying that I am a very busy executive is just an escaping answer to the cosmos. Doing such basic works connect you in all aspects of life, including health. Many locks in life will open when you do those basic domestic works.

A logical answer to such escapists is that when you eat a dish, you get to taste various tastes in the food. You get to taste sweetness, sourness, spices and various other tastes. Even if you do not get to taste all, the predominant taste remains great so you enjoy the food. Without those other ingredients in the dish, you do not get to enjoy the food. In the same way, the basic situations and fundamental way of living life with family, friends and other things are quite essential to balance the professional life. Every situation in life, weather it is with family, friends or even with a waiter in a restaurant teaches something on one hand and also burns karma on the other hand. Such situations and burning of karma actually open several locks in your business.

So simply tying yourself only to business environment always will not make you conscious of your business or always thinking about business alone does not make you conscious of your business! In fact that will hinder your personal and business progress. There are several senior executives under the impression living a false life of “always business life”. That life will not help them. It is an avoiding, preconditioned and structured life from the Nature, setting up fences around them. You are avoiding natural situations that are meant for you in this cosmic womb. Avoiding natural situations will only hinder you and your business from your actual progress.

If you cannot accept this, one day or the other, you will accept it practically as the Nature will show you the demo of it and till then you can live with your prejudices by simply saying “I am a very busy executive”.

Chapter-13

Maya or Illusion

You actually see the world with layers of lenses covered, so you do not get to see the truth. These covered layers are for the mind, not for the eyes so, after seeing, you cannot properly judge and take right decision. You see the object as snake and you do not go nearby it, but it will turn out to be rope. Then you miss the opportunity. Sometimes, you see it as rope and you approach it and then you get in trouble as it turns out to be snake! This is the vision of every man on the earth.

To get proper vision is a very long journey. Vision does not mean the vision of eye. It is the inner eye of the mind. But, you can tune to the frequency of the cosmic CEO and get his guidance from within, weather you can approach the object or not.

Maya is full of your desires, attachments and preferences that do not let you have proper vision. Most of your decisions are made based on the data of these elements said above. Some are attached to their position and its authority. Some are attached to the luxury they enjoy. Some are attached to the importance they get being in the top position. Some are attached to the respect they get and the list goes on like this. Once they enjoy these things in the world and from the people, their false self-covered with illusionary layers want these things repeatedly more and more. So to enjoy these things, they tend to do many actions and some actions go out of the way of Nature and its laws. Some even demand these things from the others. If a security guard does not salute you, you demand it by begging him to do so! There are people as such in the world who greatly enjoy such things. They further slip down to commit dangerous mistakes that hurt them and their businesses and lives very badly.

Some are madly in love with children who go to an extent of giving them all comforts by which the children may tend to do several bad actions. Such parents are afraid if losing their children, if they get angry with them and do not support their bad actions. Such fears of parents push their children into a heap of darkness that will make them do several bad actions in life. This is one kind of maya.

Some are so possessive about their belongings, which is another kind of maya.

Some always carry insecurity which is another kind of attachment that makes them not believe any person in life. They keep carrying that fear. To cover that fear, they get angry and shout. Anyone who gets angry and shouts basically they carry fears in side and they are quite timid inside. Just because they shout, they are not bold, they are actually timid inside. Their mind is weak and if they are exposed to the actual situation, their fears will come out and they present those fears to the world in the form of anger.

Maya does not let you have proper vision. It's like you are stuck in traffic, you cannot see how long the traffic is held, you cannot have proper understanding and you cannot gauge the time it could take to clear. Imagine you get onto the high-rise building nearby and see the traffic. Then you will have proper vision of the traffic and then you can gauge the time it could take to clear. You can also get to see the cause of the traffic.

But you need to get the expertise of gauging the truth being in the traffic itself, without getting onto the high-rise building. You can hire the cosmic being that can give you proper directions in such situations in life. But that energy cannot be bought or hired in technical sense. It has to be won by pure love and to follow dharma in life and business. It will work like a medicine that can be taken and from inside biologically it will start developing the proper vision and it is a journey. It will not only work like medicine but like energy that will involuntarily make you do right actions that are good for you and for your business.

Some are blinded by pride and that makes them call themselves "I am smart" and I am much smarter to others. Cheating someone, tricking someone, putting someone out of the job, disgracing others are not smart actions. Smart actions are those which do not harm you, others and the cosmos. Do not think that these are good to read in books but cannot be applied in the life. Do not think so. It is a formula, an algorithm of Nature that works not only on the earth but on any planet. You apply and see how it works. Without practically experiencing its results, you cannot simply think that way. You apply and see the kind of energy develops in you, by doing such harmonious actions.

I am very smart is a very fashionable word to say that pumps up your false ego and pride. But the actions out of such personality not only just pile up your karma that you will have to pay back to this cosmic womb but also buy you some unbearable pains.

Even great business men, out of their experiential data, they make some decisions and some of them at times fail and some of them succeed at times. But there is no guarantee that the decision will get success. Making decisions that are not out of illusion by following laws of Nature is like doing a cosmic job. Such actions will get great success and also will save huge number of people and corporations that are dependent on you. A CEO is not just a suit wearing man lost in table meetings but he is a HERO from the cosmic perspectives. He is given such responsibility, strength and mind that can shoot great arrows perfectly in the business. A CEO is a warrior of peace in a warzone sheltering several people! A CEO is given a seat of being like Arjuna.

Chapter-14

CEO Being The Hero, Arjuna

Even great warriors cannot be Arjuna. Even great experts cannot succeed as CEOs. Arjuna is an exceptional one, who represents the cutter of illusion of the matrix, The Nature. That is why he is exceptional warrior.

A CEO is supposed to be having the right vision by cutting through the illusion, with the inner eye to manage the business well.

CEO's work is just not some management of a corporation. From the cosmic perspectives, he is a hero, king and has higher responsibility in the world. So he needs to be exceptional one who can cut the illusion just like Arjuna. So every CEO is required to be like Arjuna from the cosmic perspectives. But are you, the CEO like Arjuna is a question that you need to ask yourself.

Like Neo who understands the secret of Matrix, in the movie "The Matrix", Arjuna and CEOs are like that Neo who are required to understand the algorithm and fundamental functions of Matrix, The Nature.

CEO is not just that SMART one; the way the world calls you. The worldly word of smartness is foolishness from the cosmic perspectives, because, smart worldly people act exactly the opposite way to the cosmic laws. Actual smartness is something else from the Nature perspectives. The worldly smartness is quite simple one that does not need any extraordinary thing. Extraordinary is something else that leaves the arrows perfectly in the warzone of business. It requires you to become Arjuna or Neo to leave your arrows perfectly. Arrows are shot by every normal man in the world. Shooting arrows is nothing but doing the action. But the arrow has to perfectly hit the eye of the moving fish aimed at and the same time, it should neither hurt you nor the matrix, the cosmic womb and its living contents. It requires the harmony of body, mind and soul with the exceptional shooting abilities and single mindedness.

Being Arjuna itself is difficult but he becomes more exceptional when he is guided by Krishna his friend, driver and preceptor. That is the reason why the world even after thousands of years, still remembers Arjuna. A CEO's name can also shine like that for few hundreds of years if only he becomes Arjuna. Nature can make him shine and stand out like that for many generations. That is the actual fame and name that one has to earn. Not just simply becoming

CEO for couple of decades who is forgotten by the world in just a year!

There is some basic discipline, some tapas (spiritual effort towards cosmic energies) that gets you exceptional skills and unearth unlimited potentials that can take the help of cosmic energies to manage the corporation exceptionally.

Especially in Indian region, in ancient days, even people with negative intentions, out of their spiritual practices, used to unearth exceptional potentials by which they used to become very powerful. If negative intentions earn such exceptional powers, a positive mind with pure business development interests can easily unearth such potentials. To earn such potentials, you do not have to go to Himalayas. You can earn them right there where you are currently living now with some discipline and guidance. Let me give some heads up of basic subtle body and its functions in the matrix of Nature.

You are required to understand the basic limbs and their functions of your subtle body. Your physical body has hands, legs and inside body it has liver, heart and all those. The physical body also has semi-physical and subtle organs and they are your five senses. Five senses have five subtle actions which are expressed through five action points (I am not talking about them purposely but leave them for you to think over, so do not google!).

The five senses and their subtle actions are connected to the five elements that you see in the physical world. I am sure you know five elements, which I again purposely do not want to mention.

The cosmic womb or the Nature is basically the environment of these just five elements. Every product you build, everything that you see in the world is just made out of these five elements which are directly connected to the five elements within you (which have those five subtle actions behind your five input and output organs). I purposely want to talk like this, leaving dots in between so you can fill them up on your own. So, the first step towards making you Arjuna has already started, as you read this chapter!

So, you are basically this hardware that has five input and output action points with their abilities in between. They further interact with your subtle limbs (not gross limbs of your body) MIND, INTELLECT, MEMORY, EGO and the highest capability AWARENESS.

Mind does not mean the English language related mind but it is coupled with emotions which is called Manas in Sanskrit. So we can call the mind as emotional mind, for our understanding. The mind is like a TV screen associated with its sub limb called emotion. It is the strings of the emotions that tie your mind (TV Screen) to the images that are displayed on it. Emotions are powerful because they carry energies.

Above this mind, you have intellect which purely works on logic.

Memory is another limb that stores situations, objects, their sensual data (with colors, smell etc.). Memory is purely like a database of a software. The data would be in the format of images, audio, video and senses related experiential data. Memory also stores the data based on the thoughts you process, between mind and intellect. That data may not be a practically experienced data which is realistic but it also can be stored in memory based on your thoughts which form basically opinions and beliefs.

Thc memory also stores energies of every object. For example cigarette, if you are smoker the cigarette image with its taste, smell and the experiential data written so strongly in your system. The moment you see the object "cigarette" or get its smell or you see someone smoking, immediately in fraction of seconds, the feeling of smoking awakens from your system within. Smoking is a habit that is badly written in the database of your memory with high energy. These habits are called traits. Every trait of yours, carry certain energies. Some habits carry certain energies. Those habits and their energies make you behave in the world. You cannot leave some bad habits and weaknesses (even if you know that they are bad), because of this reason. You only know few bad habits and weaknesses of yours. There are few hundreds of habits that you do not even know that they are bad. Those habits are basically the habits that function against the Laws of Nature. Because of these traits and their energies that make you act in the MATRIX, this field of world, to do your karma (actions). Some of those actions are good which generate good karma (which will give you good fruits in future) and some of those reap bad karma that gives you pains in future. Both good and bad karmas make you OWE to the cosmos, the Matrix.

The point you need to remember is, you are different and these subtle limbs are different.

You are feeling like smoking immediately right? Then, who is that YOU feeling? Is that your mind that is feeling? Is that your intellect or who is that? Let's not go to the answer yet! Let's keep this aside.

Now let us go to the limb of AWARENESS. The awareness is an apparatus that basically works so silently in the background of your senses and also within your mind when an object appears on the TV screen (mind).

The work of awareness is basically to just recognize the objects and sensual data. You see an apple and if you are hungry, then in fraction of seconds, its sensual data within you wake up and trigger your subtle data carriers and then you automatically get saliva in your mouth. Then you feel like eating the apple. The uncontrollable sensual urges with their high energies, enforce you to do certain illegal or unethical actions, which modern man lacks today. He already does not have controlling energies of those sensual demands and if is drunk or in drugs, negative cosmic energies act on him and force him to get into those actions which damage him so badly in his life forever.

There is another limb called WILL, it gives freedom to anyone to act, think and do whatever they want. That FREE WILL is the reason behind your actual soul journey.

There is main limb called EGO. EGO is a limb that recognizes you with your mind and body. This EGO is always covered and works with its closest friend “awareness” and they both actually cheat you in every interaction you have with an object in the world and its data.

The EGO with Awareness mainly works with all the lower level subtle limbs, mind, emotions, intellect, memory and then they process the thoughts so fast in micro seconds. Their speed cannot be measured by any device in the world.

Now all these limbs work like front-end, backend, database, and middle ware of a software which interact with hardware of mobiles or computers. The same mechanism happens within you.

But all these limbs are where? Where all these limbs are there, that is your actual you. From that your actual YOU, your subtle body (mind, intellect and all those subtle organs explained above) is hanging and further from that subtle body your physical body is hanging in the world.

That YOU, when, its actual journey started first time, it had all its limbs but the DATA in all those limbs was empty. It is just like when you install a new software, it would not have any data in it but it still would have front-end, backend, middleware and all those. As you start using it, you will enter lot of data into it and as per that data, the software starts behaving. In the same way, when you started your journey first, you had empty data in your soul software.

Your traits, the data you store in the memory actually make you get into actions so that you either get rid of your already accumulated karma or accumulate new karma during the process of actions. The data of your karma is also stored in your karmic records that Nature carries in its womb. Karma is not stored in any of your subtle limbs.

Now the point comes to WHO ARE YOU actually? You are actually that cosmic consciousness that is spread everywhere. Its like MAGNETISM of the magnetic field. That magnetism is you which is there in the entire field.

But your will, awareness and ego tie you to the body and mind then limit you feel and think that you are small, you are that, you are this and so on. The obligated karma is the main reason that pushes you into this magnetic field (comic womb) again and again.

Imagine that "magnetism" has intelligence and imagine that it is considering itself as the physical magnet. Physical magnet is true and it is appearing in the world, but its magnetism is the reality of it spread around in a spherical way and that magnetism is the actual doer but not the magnet. But magnetism cannot be seen. Just like that magnetism, you are thinking that you are actually the physical magnet. But in your case, magnet, which is your body, came down due to its magnetism, the soul or consciousness.

Can you show anyone what MAGNETISM is? Can you see it? All you can do to prove magnetism is by placing iron metal thing in its field. Then the magnet will do the action of attracting it. But literally you cannot show the magnetism. Magnetism has some power; it has some energy and force behind. All those three together is magnetism.

You are like that magnetism actually which is called "consciousness" or soul or Atman. That consciousness is you with all its limbs explained above.

That consciousness is the one that logs out of your body system when you fall deep into sleep. But your awareness and all its subtle limbs remain with your body. It is the awareness that works like INVOKER or CALLER of your consciousness. Awareness calls your consciousness into the body because of which you wake up alive. If awareness fails or consciousness does not come to your body, then it is called death. In sleep, your consciousness merges in its true self which is the cosmic consciousness or vast self and gets charged. Because of that charging, you feel energized after waking up. If you don't sleep for couple of days, you feel so weak because, your consciousness is not charged. Meditators who get into Samadhi, they charge their consciousness by merging it with the cosmic consciousness. They do not need sleep.

In India, they do some rituals in eleven to fourteen days after the death. The awareness of the consciousness (soul) still recognizes itself with the body, its family, friends and its place of living. That recognition will last for 12 to 14 days after the death. So, they chant some vedic mantras which instruct the soul to continue its journey by leaving this dead body and all its relations.

If the awareness still does not leave the body and its association, then such souls become ghosts. The deep desires especially associated with revenge etc. make the souls still remain with the awareness of that body. Nature, the field or the cosmic womb also supports those souls because, the souls cannot remain unsatisfied. If some injustice happens to anyone out of some crime, then Nature the cosmic womb supports those souls in its field to get justice to those souls who remain like ghosts for some time. Supporting those ghosts is also one of the works of Nature to get them justice in the real world.

So you are basically that pure consciousness.

Now let us go to the God element. God, mentioned by religions is nothing but this pure consciousness, that vast consciousness in which your small pool of consciousness is merging, when you fall into deep sleep. You are also actually that vast consciousness. You keep merging your small pool of consciousness (your limited self) in the deep sleep every day, with cosmic consciousness (your unlimited self or your true self or God).

God's consciousness is nothing but that pure consciousness which does not have any body like you. You took body because you owe the karma to the cosmos. Whereas, God does not owe anything to the cosmos, so he remains without body.

That pure consciousness is called Holy Ghost in Christianity. That is pure and unlimited whereas you are impure because of which you became limited and you keep taking bodies till you merge back into that pure consciousness by paying back all your obligated karma. Yoga system calls it freedom. You are the small particle consciousness of God's pure consciousness. Your particle consciousness logs out of your body and merges in the cosmic or God's consciousness and gets charged in the deep sleep. It is just like your Wi-Fi field of internet going away, when you turn off your router and your Wi-Fi internet field disappears by merging itself in the actual unlimited oceanic field of internet.

So you are basically that pure consciousness with all those limbs.

For your understanding all these had to be said. But it does not mean, you have understood it perfectly.

What is understanding?

Understanding comes out of experience only. So by knowing, understanding comes i.e. by experience understanding comes. Anything that does not get you experience, is just piece of information. It is not actually, understanding. Understanding comes after knowing. So where there is knowing, there is understanding.

So all that above said could get you some imagination of little understanding based on the data that you carry in your soul system.

To get this understanding fully or to the level of KNOWING, there is a big spiritual journey that has to be taken up.

That does not mean, I suggest you to take up, spiritual journey by leaving the great cosmic responsibility of CEO Job you have. You are already given a great opportunity by the cosmic governance system to play an important role in it.

You are given that opportunity but are you doing that cosmic job properly?

First of all, you do not know yourself that you are playing a role in cosmic management team. On top of it, as you do not know the truth, you are not playing your role perfectly.

Perfection does not mean, just that worldly SMARTNESS word that everyone calls so fashionably.

Real smartness is playing that role in the cosmic management team under the main CEO of GOD or whatever you call him. You can call him friend or preceptor or Big Brother or Big Boss or God or whatever and with his help, you will be able to perfectly operate and function in life and business. It is more important to you, the CEO than the common man.

Religions build faith, devotion and love towards God that actually makes your HEART soft. When the heart is soft, you cannot do bad things that are against the laws of Nature. Whatever the religion you belong to, this is the main intention and bottom line of every religion in the world. You are born in a religion to earn this softness of heart so that you can behave well in the world. But, after your education in universities and all, by adopting the modern life and various other reasons, you move away from your religious practices. Modernization actually should make you smarter in terms of falling in harmony with the laws of Nature. But that modernization you call is actually getting you into more bad habits and thus you are earning more and more weaknesses and those weaknesses will no way help you in your personal life or in your business. So the word modernization is a mask that you are wearing to engage in bad habits.

Because of that, the softness of heart itself is gone! Yes, religions form some kind of limitations. Religions actual intention is by following them, you need to go beyond them to realize the truth. It's like a rope; you take its help to go forward to know the truth. Those who are religious do not understand this actual intention of religion and those who do not know the intentions of religions also do not earn soft heart.

Those who are fanatic about their religions and those who are totally modern by leaving their religions, both are lost in the objectives of Nature the cosmic womb. Those who cross religious barriers, take up Yoga, which is the science of Nature. But in pure yoga practice also, takes some time, to earn that softness of the heart. Modern men, even if they cannot take up religious practices, they can even adopt yoga and follow some discipline that gets them softheartedness which is essential in life.

The bad thing today is that, the parents and society, teach you not to have soft heart. They say, if you have soft heart, you cannot live well in the world and you cannot fight well in the world and all those. So most of the elders are pushing the children towards getting hard hearts due to which they grow and commit all those actions against the laws of Nature.

But the actual truth and science is to be "a warrior by having the soft heart". It is possible to be like that. That is what it is, the Yogi in jeans, the monk CEO in business suit. Elders, who do not know about this and who are not capable enough to practice such harmony in life, they encourage the children to adopt hard heartedness.

I think now you understand! Nature needs now, Yogis in jeans, like warriors with soft hearts in the world. A Soft hearted warrior fights in harmony with the laws of Nature by not hurting himself and also by not hurting others. But yet he fights and he does not give up fighting!

Society taught you to have hard heart because it expected you to fight. In that case you lost soft heart which makes you commit mistakes in the world. So everyone is currently fighting in the world of life with hard heart. You should fight. You should not give up fighting but you should know how to fight with soft heart but not with hard heart!

The science explained above is a kind of Yogic system which gives you more a technical way of presentation of being "A Karma Yogi".

Soft heart carries emotions that are connected with the cosmos and all its contents. People in the real world, say, don't be emotional in business and life. It is actually a belief but not true from the cosmic perspectives. People became mechanical, functioning like machines and their actions without emotions always go against the Laws of Nature. Emotions carry very powerful energies. You should know how to manage those emotions and energies. If you know that art, you can move mountains and stop tsunamis with those energies for the welfare of others. People who say that are foolish and they basically do not have the capability of managing emotions and their energies. An arrow, a strategy, an email or a phone call can work like a powerful cosmic weapon, when they carry the right emotions with good intentions piercing any hard target. For

CEOs it is essential to know that art and that would be easy when they become Arjuna. It is not necessary for normal humans to know that art and if they know it, they will misuse its power.

So you do not have to leave your great cosmic opportunity given by Big Boss or God or Big Brother. You will have to do your duty (Dharma) by playing your role well. If you don't play your role as per the laws of cosmic corporate system, then obviously you are doing a big mistake. That mistake does not actually help your incorporation or your personal life.

So, how to play that role well? You do not know it. At the same time, you cannot now afford to learn that great unlimited subject of Yoga and practice. You do not have time for it too!

If you are CEO and obviously you would have a hot line or special phone line to communicate with your investors or board members etc. None of your employees or your directors below you has such SPECIAL HOT LINE to communicate with your board members.

In the same way, you have a great opportunity of having hotline to communicate with the BIG BROTHER or GOD or BIG BOSS, because you are his team member and you are playing vital role in his cosmic management team.

That art of communication, getting the guidance in managing your business is available to you.

Following Laws of Nature is nothing but the laws of the governance system of God or Big Brother. You do not know how to act, when to act in various situations as per the laws of Nature.

There is a possibility of loading an involuntary energy of God into you so that you perfectly act in all situations as per the laws of Nature. That loading of energy is nothing but loading of "ART OF GOD'S MANAGEMENT SYSTEM" into you.

That energy will load into you. I am not talking about some vague concepts here, you will experience in later part of this book.

Krishna explains the soul system and its structure which I explained in this chapter, to Arjuna in the middle of the battle field. Arjuna wants to pull out from his duty of fighting war by seeing his kith and kin in the enemy army (who actually have been against the laws of Nature).

Arjuna was originally hard hearted just like you. Later he becomes soft hearted by seeing all the kith and kin in the warzone. Then Krishna teaches him to wage war by having the soft heart inside.

Those who are against the laws of Nature are technically equal to dead ones from the Nature's governance perspectives. That governance is called DHARMA. God who comes in the form of Krishna who drives Arjuna's chariot in the war, asks him to kill all those enemies. They may be your kith and kin but they are against the laws of Nature. Nature gave enough opportunities for them to change but they did not change. You may have some friends and brothers working in your firm, but if they function against the laws of your company, will you not sack them? You may give them some opportunities to get strait but if they further continue the same mistakes, obviously you will have to sack them. Like Arjuna, you cannot tell your board of directors that they are your friends and brothers so you cannot sack them. You cannot also tell them that you will quit your CEO Job.

Another example is, the attachments you have such as fears, expectations, jealousy, anger, lust, greed and all those are like your kith and kin. You are attached to them. You are currently surrendered to them and you are not able to leave them out of attachment towards them. When those attachments are making you behave against the laws of Nature which are harmful to you, to your incorporation and your life, you will have to leave them. If they are leaving you, you will have to wage war on them!

Arjuna tells Krishna that he would rather quit his duty than killing his kith and kin in the enemy army. You are thinking the same now like Arjuna, while reading this text that, it is difficult to leave those attachments.

That's when this complete truth of matrix was revealed to Arjuna.

But even after revelation of all this technology, he still does not understand because understanding actually comes only after knowing. Explanations, speeches, reading books, little meditational practices that you do currently, do not get you THE KNOWING. If the KNOWER sits inside you, he can rent his energies through which you can see the actual world and act perfectly.

So Krishna tells him, you love me and tune to my frequency and then I will become the charioteer of your chariot. That means technically that, you love me, I will drive your body by being in you like energy. Meaning, I as pure consciousness as energy will guide you and make you take right actions with my energy by being in your heart – is what Krisha says. That means, if you tune to God's frequency and he can guide you and make you take actions involuntarily. Initially you may not have that faith and love for him, but as you start the journey, you will pick up those elements as you experience the results in life.

That is what I am saying, the art of god's management will enter into you like a software in the form of energy and help you with right advises and even give you energy to take right actions involuntarily. So the software of "The art of God's cosmic management" can be loaded into you gradually (not at one shot).

The mode of loading that god's software happens by tuning yourself to his frequency.

By connecting with him in his frequency, you will be able to load all those abilities into you INVOLUNTARILY without going to Himalayas and practicing high end of spirituality. But by following some basic discipline, some values and ethics, his response to your tuning would start. Unlike for those Yogis in Himalayas, this gift is given to you easily because you, as CEO are ready to act like Arjuna in the chaotic war zone of business, whose work is more essential in the active world. So, currently he is available to you more easily than for those in Himalayas!

This book will reveal the method of tuning to his frequency in the next chapters. You can practice that method for few days by which you will surely observe some changes in your life. In about 12 to 21 days, you will find some good changes in your life and later as you keep practicing it, you will be able to observe more transformation in life and business.

Chapter-15

The Driver

The cosmic driver Krishna, driving Arjuna That super natural power, whom you call God or Brother or Boss or Father, whatever, that supreme seabed of the consciousness which is spread everywhere is actually the driving force behind every living being in the cosmos.

That consciousness remains always as seabed in every being, in the center of the heart.

Children up to the age of 21, get to access it faster. People below that age; get to listen to its voice easily. Children get to hear that voice much faster. That is the reason why, children always express love and get attracted to the elders who express love for them. Because, the essence of the whole cosmos gets attracted to love. Out of just love, the parents meet physically and then you are born out of their love. Out of the energy of love, the whole creation came into existence. You start your incorporation out of love and then passion comes. There are five primary energies that come of your actual essence i.e. pure consciousness which actually help you to get prosperity in life and business.

Those five energies are 1. Energy of Dharma 2. Energy of love, 3. Energy of desire 4.Energy of knowledge then 5. Energy of action. All these energies get born out of you, whenever you create something in the world. For example, when you start your company, all these would be there inherently formed in you and purely because of those energies, the incorporation manifests in the real world. All these energies are meant for what?

The answer is prosperity. To get prosperity in your personal life, in your business and through your business you give prosperity to the people around, who work for you and also those who buy your products and services. These are the main energies within the nucleus or vast cosmic consciousness.

The same energies also are there in you always because you came out of that supreme consciousness.

The same process took place when this whole creation came to existence in the pure consciousness which is the source of all the cosmos.

A particle of that same ocean of cosmic consciousness always stays in your entire system (from limited consciousness to all the subtle organs explained in the previous chapter).

Because of that consciousness you gain cosmic energy that comes through life forces (there are five life forces and they are called pranas that actually pull the cosmic energy into your system) to sustain your whole system. That cosmic energy in you, does its basic work and remains always in watchful mode. It does its basic functional management work of operations in your body, such as breath, heart, digesting your food and converting it into energy form and so on. It will keep some required energy in you and it will transfer some part of your energy to the cosmic energy. The same consciousness also works to push out the waste in your guts. Without its basic work, your body cannot function.

That speck of consciousness is the one that logs out of your system when you get into deep sleep. It comes back into your system, when your "awareness" pings it back.

The always watchful mode of consciousness has the ability to guide you and speak to you in the form of intuition, in the form of thoughts and also in the form of voice and visuals. Children below 21 years get to access it easily unlike elders. Some of those directions, they can follow and some they do not follow.

But after the age of 21, they totally loose its access as their intellect and mind take over the major function of their system. The formed opinions, beliefs and thoughts will start overlapping the inner voice. As they get trapped more and more into karma, that accessibility gets much weaker and they totally loose its connection by the time they turn out to be thirty years old.

So, they cannot have those abilities of intuition and getting cosmic directions or divine directions. High end spiritual practitioners clear their covered layers and gain access to it. That is why they get to know some level of knowledge related to cosmos and Nature.

I do not mean, you will have to do all those spiritual practices to access it. But there is a shortcut that is known to some high end spiritual Gurus. That short cut is of "this driver". The accessibility to this driver, whom you call God, can get little easier for man based on the time and space and the weakness of the man's consciousness. At this point of time of the world, the man's consciousness is so weak and because of the responsibility of taking care of the cosmos, the driver makes the path of accessing him a bit easier, especially for the CEOs, who have vital role in the cosmic evolution.

That driver is the charioteer of Arjuna the great warrior of Mahabharat. Arjuna is quite smart in all aspects of his skills and mind with additional personality of following discipline and being in harmony with laws of Nature. So he earns the access to the driver within and also to the unlimited cosmic powers.

There were many exceptional and great warriors with super natural powers in Mahabharat, but even they could not get access to this driver purely because, they do not have heart of following the laws of Nature, the Dharma. Purely because of this, even superior ones to Arjuna had to lose their lives in the war. Even, those who had the powers of being deathless lost their lives purely because of lack of the element "DHARMA" in their personality.

DHARMA is following the law of the cosmos and whoever follows it, even a normal person can fight with any mighty power. Only Arjuna had that additional aptitude and love for Dharma, so he could get the access to the Driver. Even he had to be taught "as to how to access this driver within". Dharma is the supreme power in the whole cosmos. Whoever follows it, can stand against any power in the world, because behind him, the whole unlimited power of Nature would be there.

Krishna, the charioteer of Arjuna's chariot, represents God in human form. He had to teach him about all the science explained in the previous chapters. In addition he simply says, just leave all that technology and technical jargons, just love me unconditionally and I will drive your system.

In order to operate technically all those subtle organs of yours, you will have to take up high end of yogic practices. But when you love the driver, unconditionally, he will operate all your subtle organs. He can operate you because, as the seabed of consciousness, he is there in every living being. His supreme consciousness is already doing all the basic functions in you as explained above. In addition he can even drive you, in all aspects of your life so you can function well and prosper.

Currently all your subtle organs are not operating well. They are just functioning in multidirectional way, covered by illusion and being against the laws of Nature. You do not even know that those subtle organs exist in your system. The art of operating them properly takes few lives to learn by following a disciplined yogic system. Instead, the short cut is to HIRE THIS DRIVER, who will drive your system. I am literally speaking this language to sound his simplicity i.e. the owner of the cosmos being available to drive your car that of especially CEOs. The car is not your physical car. Car is your human system. To sound his simplicity, I had to use this word, driver.

But you cannot hire him by money, by showing off your attitude, ego or even spirituality. Hiring can happen only if you love him unconditionally and by seeking the true help from him. It is difficult to have love, faith and belief initially, but as you follow the methods given in the next chapter; those elements will build in you as you gain the benefits.

"You can hire me as your driver" was, said by him few thousands of years ago. But now, the state of the human consciousness is much weaker than that of those days. So the way of accessing the driver within has become a bit easier, because of his interest of helping the humanity, especially the CEOs.

Now the point is about, hiring that driver. Don't think, you will have to pay any money or lose your property etc.

In next chapter, you will be given couple of mantras to tune to his frequency so that the process of you, hiring him starts! But before that, you should know why you should hire him.

First of all you do not know the technical architecture and fundamental functions of your subtle organs. On top of it, you do not even know the laws of Nature, how to get in harmony with it and so on. To learn all those, a dedicated spiritual practice of few lives together, has to be taken up by surrendering to a Guru.

But, all that is available to Arjuna in business i.e. you the CEO, who, is busy in business and life. Because, as the CEO of your incorporation, indirectly being the cosmic team member of the super natural power and to become like Arjuna, you earn the easy access of him and you also have the cosmic permission to hire him.

By having him as the driver of your vehicle, he becomes driver of your personal life and also the driver of your business. Just like Sun, you will be shining all times in personal and business lives. The world knows only the great work and energy of Sun but hardly anyone knows the source of his energy.

Imagine, for how many years, Sun has been shining and so you can. You will get to know all the directions of his in the form of thoughts, in your dreams, in the form of voice from within and sudden visions in your mind.

Krishna, becoming Arjuna's charioteer is the meaning that Krishna is the preceptor of Arjuna who remains in Arjuna as sea bed consciousness and energy to drive mind, intellect and body of Arjuna. Then Arjuna would be able to perfectly leave the arrows to win the war. Human race cannot forget Arjuna and his work. He is always remembered as the combination of monk within and warrior, externally. But now, in the modern world, the war field is Business and the CEOs are given the opportunity of being Arjunas. Every CEO is given the cosmic opportunity to become Arjuna, but how many of them really can become Arjuna is the question and their names will always remembered in the mankind which is actually the love of Krishna, the preceptor.

Chapter-16

Tuning To The Preceptor

You can tune to the preceptor from within, whom the religions call God but in fact, he is your own true self.

By tuning to his frequency, his expertise, his consciousness, his energy, his all management expertise would start loading in to you like a software.

Just like the way the saliva oozes from your tongue, the essence of his like honey would ooze into your system and it is a gradual process. There is no end to this oozing process of his essence or loading of his software. It keeps loading as you keep living your life better and better in discipline which is a journey towards the perfection.

To tune to his energy, you do not have to take up any monastery or monkhood. You can live your normal life but with some discipline you can make the oozing much better as the discipline will get better and better in you automatically.

You can tune to his energy by just chanting the mantra which works like tuning to a radio station. Mantra is the frequency and the radio station is the super natural power, Krishna or Hari or Vishnu, the cosmic CEO.

I present you couple of mantras that will help you tune to Krishna, the super natural power, easily.

One is a simple mantra that you can chant all times i.e. while you walk, drive, cook and all in the background, silently in the mind.

The first simple mantra is this, which you can chant all times - Hari Om

You can chant this mantra all times (except in loo) in the mind like – hari om, hari om, hari om, hari om....

Mantra means, it carries the cosmic energy. It is not a mere lifeless mantra. Several people, individuals, business men, spiritual seekers, students chanted this mantra and experienced the prosperity in their lives.

Hari means, the supreme consciousness which is spread everywhere in and out of every living and nonliving beings. Hari is the seabed of the cosmic consciousness, which is there deep within you. Religions call that consciousness as God.

God is Hari whose main responsibility is sustenance of this whole creation which is nothing but the management of the whole creation. He works closely with Nature, his governance system of the cosmos. He has a huge corporate management team of divine energies who are like Sun, Moon, Five Elements, Rain Energy and so on. They all work for him and he is the source of giving energy to them so that they can perform their duties.

Once you start tuning to him, you will also become like Sun, playing a cosmic role. He is the same source of energy so that you, as CEO, can perform your cosmic duty of managing your corporation in harmony with the Laws of Nature.

In this mantra, you basically hail that Cosmic CEO, Hari.

Hari took the form of Rama when, the earth was out of the way in terms of Dharma. Hari, the CEO comes down to fire fight the problem that Nature faces (especially human consciousness). In the whole cosmos, human body is the best vehicle for any soul to evolve faster and it is human who can use the subtle organs at best to evolve his consciousness. Human consciousness plays vital role in the whole cosmos and its harmony. So, whenever there is problem in Nature, he comes down, puts back mainly the human consciousness in harmony and goes back. Just like your business, the earth would have various problems. You only get to see the GROSS PROBLEMS. But the subtle problem is the main reason for the gross problems. So he comes and mainly hits the subtle layer of human consciousness. Then, the subtle minds and gross bodies of humans naturally fall in place.

You can chant this mantra all times, anywhere (except in loo). You do not even need to count the chanting of the mantra. You can chant this mantra in mind silently while you are on treadmill, while walking in parks, while driving, while cooking and so on.

If you quit eating meat, (meat, fish and all living beings) it would be a good start. Any other bad habits that you currently have naturally will go away after starting this mantra chanting. You will find the changes happening in life, in 12 to 21 days after starting the chanting of this mantra. The transformation keeps improving as you keep chanting this mantra more and more.

You may find some visuals or voices in dreams or sometimes, some ideas or thoughts suddenly dropping into your mind, after starting this mantra chanting. Those are basically hints for you to act in your life. As the chanting improves, you will find your intuition improving more and more and then you will start hearing some voices from inside talking to you and giving directions. If not voice, while doing some action, you will get thoughtful directions, which suddenly drop into your mind.

If you have some series of thoughts running in your mind related to a specific point, in the middle of those thoughts, you find the thought of Hari, dropping into your mind suddenly like a flash. You can note that thought and follow as you want.

If you do not understand those hints, you can post your questions on the website, monkceo.net. You will be given answers for your queries. You can also email at chanthariom@gmail.com

The Mantra Hari Om means – that hari, the supreme consciousness itself is OM, the supreme source of all cosmos.

As you chant this mantra in mind, you will find that every sound in the world as OM. If you chant this mantra in mind while eating, you find the eating sounds, like OM. What is that which is finding that sound as OM? It is your awareness which is one of the main tools of the consciousness, finds it as OM.

Awareness is the superior tool of every being. It works naturally high in human beings. But, when you chant Mantra like this, it will awaken and work even much superior way. When awareness works well in you, you will excel in all things that you do in your life.

You will excel in your business and in every work you do. Your consciousness which works like shadow behind the awareness expands in the world. You will find, your mind getting sharper day by day. You will find your mind being centered and getting one-pointed naturally and effortlessly. That is the work of Hari, Krishna who is the supreme driver of your consciousness. You will be able to navigate and pick the series of thoughts that are running in your mind. Mind will start becoming more like crystal clear.

When your consciousness expands your intuition gets much sharper. You will get to know things that are happening in your world. Your world is where your awareness goes. For most of the people who are busy in their professions, their awareness remains in their professional works. Where your awareness goes that becomes your world. If you are CEO, obviously your world mostly is your business. Where your awareness goes, there, your consciousness follows. As you were already told, the consciousness is like that magnetism with power and energy. When your consciousness follows the awareness of thoughts running in your mind, then you can instruct the order of things in your mind as you want. Then, they will start materializing in the real world.

When you chant this mantra, the universal power merges with your consciousness and wherever your awareness goes; if you want any works to happen then, those works will automatically materialize in the world. The materialization happens because of the cosmic energy that is merged in your consciousness. For example, when you spend with some friends or family on a weekend, you will find that the thoughts related to that weekend and all those folks, further following you for couple of days. Your awareness will also follow those thoughts and you think further about them. As you get busy in your work, those thoughts will go away naturally. So that is how the awareness and consciousness work together. Maybe some of those thoughts would be useless for your life and profession. Such thoughts simply eat up your energies of consciousness. So, that eating up of energies is like draining out your energies which are neither useful to you or to the world. In the same way, if you watch a movie, thoughts related to that movie also will haunt you for few hours or even for a day. Such thoughts are useless.

So you should be careful about what you feed to your senses, especially to eyes. Eyes capture bigger data than other senses. Carrying unnecessary data in your system is like carrying big baggage or big data on you head. The data should always be coming from cloud. If the data comes from cloud, then, you can use it and leave it without carrying it on your head. Your system can be trained with such operational mechanisms of your senses. You will find such techniques at Hariom online transformation school for entrepreneurs at www.hariom.life

So basically the mantra Hariom helps you make your awareness more powerful and expand your consciousness. That means your subtle system remains more active. The subtle system is like a shadow behind all the data that your senses perceive throughout the day. What you see or what you read or what you hear is what you believe mostly.

Imagine, you read an email about some wrong thing happening in one of your branches of your business. You think about solutions to fix that problem, as a CEO. Your body is real in the physical world. For a software it is its code which is the source of its operation. The software may work on a computer but its truth is there in the source code. In the same way, your trueness is your source code, which is your consciousness and its subtle contents. When you chant this mantra, your consciousness pulls energies from the cosmos. Then it becomes more and more powerful day by day. You can follow certain techniques by which you can consciously order the way of things in your business and they start manifesting the real world. You can get to know all those techniques at hariom online transformation school at www.hariom.life

Now let us come back to the business problem in a specific branch. You think about some solutions and then you may sleep. But even in the sleep, even if your body is asleep, the consciousness which is always awake, continues to work in the background. It might even travel to the physical branch and see the people there and it will even identify a solution for the problem. Then, with the help of the cosmic energies, the solution will also be written or fed in your system while you are asleep. Your body may experience all this process like a dream. You will feel it is like a dream for few days. But later you will start understanding slowly that it is actually your consciousness that is working. Because in that dream, if you drink coffee, you will feel its taste, heat, happiness of drinking it and all. Soul feels happy. That happiness you will find even after waking up. You will initially think how it is possible, like this. But all these are possible and you will start understanding this science slowly out of experience.

Coming back to the problem, the Super Natural power, as you are chanting that mantra will write a solution into your system while you are asleep. You will find that, some story has happened while you were asleep. But you cannot remember it nor talk about this to others. During that day or in the next following days, you will naturally implement that solution that was loaded by the super natural power. May be during the implementation process of that solution, while you talk to some people or email them, you will suddenly experience it like a deja vu, as if you already knew it earlier.

But as you start living life like this, you will find that, some supernatural power is helping you behind your actions in the world.

To experience all this, you do not have go to Himalayas, you can just get all these while you still live your normal life by chanting this mantra in the mind.

The more you chant this mantra, the more your consciousness and its awareness get active and get integrated with the cosmic energy.

You will understand the science and technology of this mantra, as you read this chapter further.

The second mantra is – Hari Om, Hare Kalki, Hare Rama, Hare Krishna, Hare Hare.

As the second mantra is a bit long one, you can chant this mantra, when you comfortably sit at one place. You don't have to count the chanting of the mantra. Even if you sit and watch TV, you can still chant this mantra silently in the mind. You can also chant this mantra while walking, cooking etc in the background. Based on comfort, you can either chant this mantra all times or chant only when you sit.

Do not worry that you need to be so disciplined and chant in meditation etc. You can chant in meditation too, if you are used to meditation. If not, you can so casually chant this mantra.

Do not worry about discipline etc. Discipline needs to come into you automatically, but not forcibly. Forcible discipline does not sustain long. Your system wages war against the forcible discipline. So first get the system used to the mantras, by simply chanting. In few days and months you will find changes automatically happening in your system. You will find discipline falling in place naturally without any war from within. So casually start chanting these two mantras. But do not chant this mantra in loo. There are several people who could quit smoking, drugs and all after starting this mantra chanting.

Now let me explain about the meaning of this mantra.

You already got to know about Hari Om and its meaning in the first mantra. The same meaning of it follows even in the second mantra. Now, let me explain the other parts of the second mantra.

HARE KALKI – Kalki is the incarnation of God and this incarnation of God is yet to take place in the world and it is meant to happen at the end of the current time and space of the world, which is called Kali Yuga. Incarnation of God is simply like a version of the same software. It comes with various additional features as the users need those features.

Every incarnation of God takes place to adjust certain ingredients in Nature. Jealousy, anger, lust, greed, following discipline, not misusing the authority etc. form the human characteristics that play vital role in the holistic Nature. You cannot take one man and his characteristics alone. These characteristics are like ingredients of a dish, like salt, sourness, sweetness, spices and all. Nature takes all humanity and based on the analysis done, it will come to a conclusion that so and so characteristics are playing more role in the world. Based on the time and space, which is era, certain ingredients of humanity are allowed by the Nature for its evolution. If those ingredients go out of balance in a major way, such imbalance causes big problem for the sustenance of the Nature and its governance system. Nature tries to adjust these ingredients on its own, for a certain period. Just like one of your limbs, if it does not function well in the body, it will try to adjust for some time and later when it goes beyond certain level, your body will start experiencing pains. That is when, you will see a doc. In the same way, Nature tries to adjust itself for some time which could be few hundreds of years. To bring balance, Nature also brings down various souls such as Spiritual Gurus, Saints etc to the world who will bring some shift. Even then, if the expected shift does not happen, then just like the way it happens in your corporation, the owner or the CEO himself will have to jump into the situation to fix the problem. In the same way, the pure consciousness, the supreme self has to take a body and jump into the world to fix a serious problem in creation. This is how the supreme incarnation takes place. When he comes down, he might work in a specific region of the world, but that work would have impact in the whole world which is the beauty of his work. His consciousness technically remains everywhere in and out of everything and every being in the world. Because of that, his work in one region or one corner of the world with some human bodies will bring transformation in the entire world. In the ancient days, kings used to rule various regions in the world and that was the way things were in order those days. When Krishna came, he created a small city called Dwaraka in the Indian Ocean and there he implemented a kind of democratic government system. That was the first time, democracy was implemented in the world. It was done almost 5000 years ago. Though it was not a perfect democracy, but the intention of the supreme consciousness continued its work, even after his leaving the earth and today, in the world, most of the countries have democratic governments. It was implemented few thousands of years ago like a model, which was then, actually meant for future generations to come. That is how the shift comes in the Nature.

When it comes to Kalki, before his actual physical appearance which will take place few hundreds of years later, but his soul work has started preparing the world to evolve in terms of consciousness. Following laws of Nature and having love in every aspect of his actions, man lack currently in his system.

Kalki means it's a software, the supreme consciousness with certain features that are required to manage the cosmos, especially human consciousness of the current age. As per the need of the Nature, his software is given the management responsibility to rule the current phase of the world. So his management is reaching all four segments of the human society i.e. 1. Spiritual Gurus 2. Politicians and federal administrators 3. Entrepreneurs and 4. Professionals and common man and. As part of his new management operations, his energy is open to work with all these four segments of the society to get involuntary transformation and prosperity.

Almost every man is living against the laws of Nature in the current world. Love is misunderstood and taken for personal carnal pleasures and taken only for family and other close members. Love in attachment is misunderstood as True Love. No one works out of love for the work. Pure love is the essence that actually gets superior experience to the people. That superior experience alone will satisfy the souls and that satisfaction alone will kill their karma. That satisfaction alone adds value to the material world. But that essence is lost in human consciousness now.

Dharma or following laws of Nature is the main ingredient of cosmic supreme soul. It is like the male source and later Love falls in place from where the creation takes place. Love is also just an ingredient as said earlier. But Dharma is not an ingredient like salt, spices etc. We can eat food at times, even if salt is less and even if other spices are not there. We cannot eat anything if the basic element of food itself is not there. That is called "Dharma". Dharma is the base element which is always there in the supreme consciousness. When it intends to form the creation, then love, desire, knowledge and action come as other main ingredients in creation. But all those come after the main ingredient called Dharma. Dharma itself is yoga and yoga itself is dharma. It means harmony, balance in all aspects of mind, intellect and actions of body.

If that basic element itself is at its stake, then obviously there is a serious issue in the world's consciousness. It's like tissues in your skin or any material, if that tissue itself is not there, then the material itself does not exist. That bad phase has already started in the world and the next generations are going to go through worse situations in life, on the earth.

So Kalki's supreme soul work mainly takes place to bring Dharma and Love into the human consciousness. If these two are there, rest all harmony will fall in place automatically in the human consciousness. So he exercises mainly with top order of people in the society as said earlier. If the transformation happens in them first, then obviously the people below them will change. Just chanting the mantra of his will bring transformation in the personalities of the top order people in the society. They not only transform in terms of personalities, they will be greatly supported by Cosmic Energies to guide people below them. They will be given all required facilities, material comforts, success, authority and all, in order to lead the people below them well. That's why their duties are not personal duties but they are cosmic duties for the welfare of the world.

Kalki's supreme soul personality is so perfect with all needed qualities of today's man in the middle of all technologies. It is like you can say, the latest version of God Software that is ready to deal with today's problems in this modern world. Because of negativity in the world, its virus software also has its latest version. It has its own strategies to damage all people in the world by introducing them to all types of bad habits. To deal with the negativity and its severity, the suitable antivirus is needed which is the version of "Kalki". So, by chanting this name, you will be mainly loaded with Dharma and Love software versions which have several other ingredient-energies that help you manage your duties so well. With high end of cosmic knowledge, his software helps you cut all negativity so that you can lead all the people in a supreme way. Today, in every company, you see verities of negativity in people that are lagging the progress of the incorporation behind. Normal intelligence cannot deal with such negativity. It requires supernatural antivirus with some extraordinary expertise. That can happen by taking the help of cosmic energies. CEOs especially, with the help of this latest version of the supernatural characteristics of Kalki, they will be able to effectively deal with such negativity.

In Rama's campaign, Dharma was given more importance and in Krishna's campaign, Love was given more importance and this time, in the campaign of Kalki, it would include both Dharma and Love. When they happen both hand in hand at the same time, the evolution would be quite faster. Kalki though he is yet to appear on the earth, his spiritual divine energy has already taken its responsibility as the Cosmic CEO of the current time and space. His consciousness and energy has started working in the spiritual plane of the human consciousness to prepare the ground for his appearance. Shree Maha Avatar Babaji, the ancient sage, who is still available in the form of soul in Himalayas, has done tremendous amount of work to bring the super natural power, of Kalki down to the earth, for the welfare of the humanity.

Every incarnation would have its pre appearing ground work, done on the earth. Hariom Movement is such call to the divine energy to speed up the human evolution. In future the humanity is going to go through several problems and you will be part of it. You cannot avoid this by saying; "I will not face those problems". You will again login to this same cosmic womb, as you owe to this womb. Some of the elders and great thinkers always say "for our next generations" which does not mean there will be others in that next generations! It is you, who is going to again take body and login to this cosmic womb. What you do today is what you are going to go through tomorrow.

The cosmic womb and its environment is going to have many issues in it during which, the humanity will have very bad time. The call to Hare Kalki is the mantra that will let you sail through that tough time easily and its call will reduce the tough time (the current age, Kaliyuga) and its span so that you, who will be part of next generations, will be able to get though that tough time easily. The call to Hare kalki will get away all negative energies around you and secure you or protect you from them and at the same time, it will transform you from within that will help you to prosper in personal life and business.

Next part of the mantra is Hare Rama.

HARE RAMA - Rama came down, when there was a big problem for mainly monk spiritualists who play the main role in evolution of human consciousness. Nature wants them to do their job so that, there can be balance in it. What is good for Nature is the Dharma. Letting monk spiritualists doing their duty is DHARMA, of every man on the earth. If some monks are doing their spiritual rituals, others should not disturb them and stop them from doing their duties. Monk spiritualists and their duties are very essential in the Nature. Their works basically bring lot of balance in Nature and human consciousness.

In the Indian sub-continent, those days, spiritual monks were invaded by negative energies and they used to kill many monk spiritualists simply to take over the land. So, Rama came down and waged war on all those negative energies and saved the spiritual monks. Then, they could perform their spiritual duties which brought balance in Nature.

Rama's work basically campaigns about "dharma" in life. Dharma is discipline, living in harmony with the laws of Nature. His work campaigns mainly following DHARMA in life. Do actions that are good for the Nature and the whole human consciousness was his campaign. He lived his life like a normal human as a married man and showed the way of following the "laws of Nature" to humanity, through all his difficult times. How difficult ever the situations were, he never quit, following the "laws of Nature" in his life. Though he was super natural power, he did not use those powers in fighting the negative forces, those days. He wanted to show the world that, when you follow the dharma, “laws of nature”, in your life, that discipline itself earns greater energies for you to defeat any kind of mighty power. Stick to the laws of Nature in all difficult times and fight. Then, your enemy will naturally go against the “laws of Nature” which becomes your strength. Then the whole Nature and its supernatural energies stand by you to defeat him – This is what Rama showed to the world practically.

The next part of the mantra is Hare Krishna.

HARE KRISHNA - In the same way, Krishna came down, when the human consciousness had the problem of Dharma again. This time he wanted to hit the main source of Dharma which is love. Love is the source of discipline, following law, to speak and interact with people well and to live in harmony with the laws of Nature. This is the soft heart, I earlier talked about. If love is there in its first place, rest all will fall in place naturally. He accompanied with his counterpart Radha, who is the symbol of love which is the essence of human consciousness. He worked with her to bring back love in human consciousness. Because of lack of love in its place, the dharma (following laws of Nature) got disharmony with the cousins of the then ruling king’s family of a region in India. Due to that, the war of Mahabharat took place which balanced love element in human consciousness those days.

So, Krishna’s campaign to the humanity was “love”. If love is there in every action you do, the other needed ingredients in personality, will fall in place naturally. If love is there in your work, your work will start speaking and it will carry some energy. If love is there in your speech, you will attract others and others will follow you. Business or every creation comes into place just out of love. Business is a dream or love of an entrepreneur. This is the reason why, in businesses, you hire ladies to interact with customers mainly. Because, their actual nature is speaking softly to the people and love is their true nature because of which they are naturally like that. But today, even they are spoiled which we cannot discuss much now, as it is a subject of huge ocean by itself!

Business does not mean mainly money making machine. Money making is a byproduct of the love or dream of the entrepreneur. That is why you will always find difference in "entrepreneur" being CEO and the professional CEO. The dreamer of a dream only knows the sweetness of the dream. The seers of the dream are always out of the dream and they only see it as a story without emotions. Let this product be helpful to the people of the world – is the dream and love of the dreamer or the entrepreneur. That's where his dream or creation starts from. Rest all fall in place, out of rational plan and strategy of the business man. How much ever strategy he applies, he always applies only constructive strategy that helps his dream to manifest. But his strategies would never try to harm the people of the world.

Because the love from where he started his dream, that always runs in the background making him to work only on the positive side, to help people but not to trick people and deceive them, with his creation. That compassion is always carried in the heart of the dreamer. That is why the creator of the business, as he retires and when the business changes hands to next generations, the operational style of the business will change. It might become more like a mechanical operation of business without ingredients of love and compassion. His children or followers did not dream that business so they do not know the sweetness and love side of it.

The soft heartedness mentioned in earlier chapter comes into picture at this point. Softheartedness needs to be there in every human and it is not a weakness. Sadly it is considered as weakness in the modern world and even in the modern business world. Because they do not know how to FIGHT in life having soft heart, most of the people have taken up the route of hard heartedness or not having heart at all in their actions. They have given a MASK to their weakness by saying "emotions are not good in life and business". So they only apply intellectual minds which only have logic but do not consider laws of Nature. So they do all actions against the laws of the Nature and most of the times fail but inside they keep crying for their actions. Technically on the long run, they are losing and hurting themselves. This sad part is bought by all modern people and they are living their lives with that belief.

Emotion is required in the actions. Emotion is the actual energy that works behind your actions, coupled with intentions. If there is no emotion in your action, it is like attacking with a dead weapon. Emotion can be used badly with bad intentions to cause destruction as well. But you should know how to use emotions. The incapability of using emotions have made the modern man to totally avoid it in his life saying "don't be emotional" which is making him mechanical, energyless and to do negative actions against the laws of Nature. It's like drunkards. When a man wants to do bad action in life, he takes liquor and does. Because, he cannot face his consciousness without alcohol. His consciousness says always don't do such bad actions, so he kills it by taking liquor and does all those bad actions. Society calls that man, a thief or a murderer and all based on the bad actions he does.

The point is, what is the difference between that man and a normal man who kills his emotions? That bad man also has killed his emotions or conscience by taking liquor and you also kill your emotions of conscience with the modern word "Don't be emotional". Don't be emotional has to be more applied to bad actions that harm the world and others but not for good actions that expand your consciousness.

Your conscience cries inside when you do not follow dharma means, whenever you do actions against the laws of Nature, your conscience naturally cries inside. But you kill it with modern word, “don’t be emotional”. Man does not have enough soul energies to manage and control emotions. In fact ordinary people do not need that expertise and art. But CEOs who are in cosmic role, need the art of managing emotions for which they need high end of soul energies. They can earn those cosmic energies with the help of the driver “Krishna”. They can apply that art like a weapon for constructive purposes. Ordinary people need not know that art as they can misuse that power!

Krishna came exactly to teach this element in the world. You should have soft heart and yet you should fight. It is like you should know karate but use it for your defense and if the fight is not avoidable, the objective of the fight should be only to defeat the opponent but not to hurt or kill the opponent! That aspect has to be adopted in real life. This is what Krishna’s campaign. You can execute it well, when you take the help of Krishna, the driver.

Soft heart is never a weakness but it is a great cosmic element that gives cosmic energy to win any kind of wars without even fighting the wars!

So Krishna’s campaign was, “have love in every action and every interaction you do”.

The last part, in the mantra is Hare Hare. It addresses the whole meaning of the mantra. The meaning of the mantra is - Hari is Om and Om is

Hari. That means Hari is God and God is Hari. The incarnations of Kalki, Rama and Krishna are nothing but of God, Hari.

So putting all these three cosmic energies together, this mantra – Hari Om, Hare Kalki, Hare Rama, Hare Krishna, Hare Hare - offers the complete package of love and dharma in its cosmic software with all required management expertise and other skills for the CEOs.

Now the question comes, how do I visualize the mantra in the form of God and what would be his form? You can either visualize the form of the God or without even visualizing the form of the God, you can chant these two mantras.

Candle light or Indian lamp is the form of the formless-form of God. Any soul is basically seen or treated in the form of candle light or Indian lamp. That is the reason why, at holy places and when people die and you find candle lights.

You will naturally find lot of peace and happiness, even at your candle light dinners. That is the sign of spirit.

So you can visualize that form of God, in case you want any form of it and then chant the mantras as said.

Chanting the mantra does not cost you anything. The human rational mind cannot perceive certain things in the creation. To experience the results, you can test by chanting these two mantras for at least 21 days. It works like a formula and you can experience the results of it, when you apply it. So be positive and try chanting these two mantras and see what will happen in next few days!

You can share your experiences on the website, monkceo.net. If you have any questions related to your thoughts or dreams etc, you can post them on monkceo.net website or you can also email at chanthariom@gmail.com

This mantra is just an initial step that starts your transformation. There are few other mind level practices that you can follow to load the software of the preceptor more, so you prosper in life and business involuntarily. An online transformation school is available at hariom.life website, which you can practice from home and experience transformation and prosperity in life. If you are interested to take up online workshop, you can check the details on the monkceo.net or hariom.life websites.

Chapter-17

Karma Vs Universal Karma

Universal Karma is the job done by the divine universal personalities such as Sun, Five Elements and all. Saints, monks, Spiritual Gurus are into doing universal karmas. It does not mean they do not have any physical comforts in life. Sun has a kingdom to enjoy the benefits of his universal duty and so are all. So, do not misunderstand that the universal personalities are there only to sacrifice but not to gain anything in life. It is a wrong understanding and opinion or belief in the society. By doing their universal karmas, by default they gain the material benefits in life, in terms of money, authority, recognition, people working for them, not having failures in their works, always seeing only success in their works and so on. These are all the benefits of the universal personalities who perform their duties as per the laws of Nature. In fact they shine more than normal humans as they have cosmic energies supporting them.

Politicians, CEOs, administrators, professors, teachers in society are also given the same opportunity by the Nature to do the universal works. They do not have to do any additional universal works in specific. By just doing their duties as per the laws of Nature, they would by default, play universal role in the Nature. All these are actually universal personalities.

Their karmas or actions are for the welfare of others. Their actions are not meant to happen out of their attachments. The duties they perform are for the welfare of others. But in the process of doing universal works, they shine big way unlike normal humans. They can shine like the Sun. The recognition they get, the people they have around, the kind of cosmic energies they carry and the kind of impact they bring in people around etc. come to them based on the selfless duty they perform. Performing that universal duty is a kind of commitment and a kind of sacrifice for the welfare of the world and people. That personality is universal personality. That personality is quite vibrant, energetic, bold and fearless personality. That personality carries the love and compassion for the welfare of others. But it does not mean that is a weakness as explained in the earlier chapters.

Even great personalities who want to do universal works, they wait for such opportunities to come. The opportunities do not come to them so easily.

Politicians, CEOs, federal administrators, teachers and professors naturally get such opportunity. It is an opportunity given to them by the divine.

Everyone cannot get that opportunity. You as CEO, are given that opportunity because, your incorporation plays a vital role in the evolution of human consciousness by giving the souls a platform where they burn their karmas.

But the given opportunity and living with that duty is more challenging and that demands universal energies to sustain in that position. You cannot sustain with weak personality in the CEO position.

The cosmic CEO, who is God, works with those who are into doing universal works. Just like the energy behind the Sun, every CEO and all the other personalities said above, in the society have the opportunity to carry the cosmic energy behind. But how many CEOs and all those personalities carry the cosmic energy is the question.

The world is at a bad cycle of time and space that actually does not allow them to do their duties well. Most of them go away from the universal laws and commit several mistakes out of their attachments, personal gains and fears. They carry such weak personalities because they are NOT AWARE that they are actually supported by the huge cosmic force that cannot be defeated by any worldly energy. But if they know that they are backed by such cosmic force, then some of them might definitely come forward to perform their universal duties in harmony with laws of Nature.

Not even great spiritualists are given such opportunity to do cosmic jobs but CEOs get that opportunity naturally.

You as CEO, you can get to know that you are backed up by the cosmic CEO or God and his immense energy, by tuning to his frequency. You can experience his immense energy by chanting the mantras given.

As you chant the mantras, the Management Software of the CEO of the cosmos with his unlimited energies will load into you and it is a gradual process. Chanting the two mantras given is the first step of the transformation process.

Normal people do karma or actions for their personal gains. So their benefits will always be limited and small. They usually live with their own weaknesses.

There is a huge difference between normal man and the CEO who has the capacity of Arjuna. Even every CEO cannot become Arjuna. CEOs are given the opportunity of becoming Arjuna and only after becoming Arjuna one can perform the universal work just like The Sun, other cosmic elements and divine energies.

It does not mean, I am saying you as Arjuna do not get any personal benefits. Personal benefits are byproducts of the universal work. The benefits will anyway come and when you do the cosmic job the personal benefits will be much bigger than what normal people get. The difference between the actions of normal people and the CEO is this way – Normal people work with the aim of personal gains and thus they get limited personal benefits. CEOs work for the cosmos and their job earns them much bigger benefits than normal people.

Another point is every CEO cannot be ready to become Arjuna despite being given the cosmic job opportunity of doing universal karma. Only few CEOs scale up to that level and live with such responsibility and they are called "Monk CEOs". They will be forever remembered in the history of business world. They are like Shiva and Shakti or Radha and Krishna like half Yogi and half CEO. If you imagine walking on water, they walk on the water but as they walk, they neither sink in water nor fly in the air! They are quite sharp with the management of divine expertise and divine energies! They are much superior to those Gurus who set up ashrams and teach yoga and all. Such CEOs actions radiate in the womb of the cosmos that will shine like The Sun.

In the earlier chapters of this book, I mentioned that, it is Nature that works behind all movements of people. It is its force that is behind the positive actions of the people. Nature meets people based on their karma and it is one of the responsibilities of Nature. All this knowledge was shared in the earlier chapters.

That force of Nature will work behind you and your entire corporation, once you, the CEO become Arjuna, then the whole Nature and its energy will work for you. As Arjuna, because your job gets universal, what you intend, what you think will be manifested in your business by the Nature.

These are like some divine miracles which happen, as your own true self starts getting divine.

Chapter-18

Dharma

Dharma means, doing actions that do not disturb Nature. Dharma means, the true-beingness of the soul or the true-self. Original trueness knows what it is. But your original trueness has lost its quality due to karma and traits. On top of it, your mind and intellect do not allow you to be your own true-self.

The essence of the soul is love and it knows perfectly how to act at every situation and it knows the trueness and true perception of it, because of which, it acts well.

Even great sages who know the operations of all the subtle organs of human personalities do not know at times, how to act as per the Dharma. The true-ness knows and experiences its actual true self with the integration of all living and non-living beings.

Your true-self knows that, it is in all and all are in it. When you know your true-self you will actually hang from it and perceive the whole world from it. You don't perceive it from the senses and the body.

However, since you cannot easily experience your true-self, with the help of the frequency tuned to the cosmic CEO, you will be able to experience it to certain extent and it lets you perceive the world with connectedness. That connectedness actually makes you think and act well in the world.

Dharma cannot be written in books. Dharma itself is truth and dharma itself is God. You cannot differentiate the government and governance from the ruler of it. The ruler's essence and laws are found in his governance. So that way, Dharma itself is God. The word Dharma is closer to the word, values.

In simple way to say, if you see yourself in others and act, then you act perfectly act as per the dharma or laws of the Nature.

If you see yourself in your customer, you will deal with him perfectly. When you see yourself in your employees, you deal with them perfectly. How do you see yourself in others you may ask. You are already doing that in case of your children or parents.

If your children eat well, you feel happy about it. If your children have comforts, you feel good about it. If your son or daughter buys a big car and drives it, you feel happy, even if you do not own it or drive it. If your son gets a good job, you feel happy about it. How do you get that happiness? You get that happiness, because you see yourself in your children. But currently, that is remaining with your children only and it is not extending to other relations in the world. Even if your business is not doing well and your friend's business is doing well, you don't get jealous of his success.

If you see yourself in others, even if the other person gets angry with you, you don't lose your temper.

But when you see yourself in others, you may also accept the mistakes of others. But the truth is, accepting and supporting the mistakes of others is not good. So, seeing yourself in others should not make you weak in terms of opposing their mistakes. You should stand up against the mistakes they do and fight.

It's like you see yourself, in children but if your children commit some mistakes, will you not tell them? If you support them or your silence can make them get much worse later. You see yourself in your children, but it does not mean, you accept the mistakes they do. The mistakes not only hurt them, but also the world. So, someone being in discipline to not to commit mistakes is in a way called, Dharma. It is also dharma, when you stand up against the mistakes of others.

Say your friend gives you a job. You are living by the job he has given you. You can be thankful to your friend for that. But if your friend does some mistakes and if he asks you to do some mistakes, you should tell him that, "you are ready to leave the job but you cannot commit the mistakes he asked to do". That way, you stand by the Dharma. Dharma does not mean, just because your friend gave a job, you get to do whatever he says. Giving value to friendship is good but that friendship should not let you commit crime and other things such as cheating others and so on, which harm others.

Following your responsibility and duty is also dharma. You as CEO are universal being who gets to see all employees the same way. You cannot do favors to some and you cannot trouble others. That becomes like misusing the authority you have. Just because you are a CEO, you cannot misbehave or misuse your authority.

At this juncture, I would like to remember one of the god's incarnations called "Parasurama". He was a pious man doing his spiritual practices. He gets born in a sect called Brahmanas. That sect is meant to live life in spiritual practices to know the God. But when the king of that region commits a big mistake against the laws of Nature by misusing his authority, he fights with him. Being spiritual, with his very high end of energies, he, not only fights with that king but later, he will go after correcting all kings and their way of ruling in the entire Indian subcontinent. In his incarnation, he used to literally kill all kings whoever committed big mistakes that were against the laws of Nature. Kings literally used to live in disguise wearing women clothing.

Here, you see, the spirituality or soft heartedness is not at all a weakness to Parasurama. But it was his strength. So he waged war on all kings who misused their authority.

Committing serious mistakes that actually harm others by misusing authority is a big crime in terms of laws of Nature. Few of such mistakes would be accepted by the Nature, by giving the opportunity for you to change. If those mistakes get worse, the Cosmic CEO's energy will manifest in some body of the world. It will come and see the end of such people who acts against the laws of Nature. Dharma works like an algorithm. It does not care if it is your mother, father or son. It works the same for all.

That incarnation of God killed many kings but that killing brought lot of balance and harmony in the Dharma of the world related to "using authority in proper way". But God killing all kings should not be misunderstood that he did mistakes. There has to be someone to clean the system when the system gets worse beyond its limitations. Nature is like a TREE and if its system gets worse, it will cut its own branch. Else, the disease will spread to other branches and to the whole tree. So Nature, The tree would manifest its energy in someone, who comes and cleans up the system. The cleaning at times would be sweet, nice and at times it would be quite painful and wrathful.

So following Dharma is very essential for everyone who is living on the earth, especially for the CEOs who have the cosmic job of taking care of their incorporations.

The mistakes of ordinary people, employees etc. can be forgiven by the Nature and the Nature gives more time for them to correct themselves. In case of

CEOs and other top order of people in the society, Nature would act quite fast in correcting their mistakes. Sometimes the correcting actions of Nature would be smooth and at times quite rough.

Committing mistakes is accepted by the Nature as its law considers it as an opportunity given to the doer, to correct him. If he continues with those mistakes, then Nature's energy would manifest in some form. You don't have to see him as God. If human body is not available, it can even come in any animal form also and take action. If not them, it can manifest through five elements in the form of earthquakes, tsunamis, hurricanes etc. In such cases, it will totally erase huge number of people, not just one or two. Man being in discipline is Dharma. So he should always remain in his discipline by keeping his ego aside. Ego is hit big time, in case of committing mistakes. You can easily understand some people trying to correct you by giving some alarms. Even if those alarms are not cared, then Nature will manifest its energies in some form to see the end of such person and his actions.

For the laws of Nature, it does not matter, if you are a man or animal or if you belong to some sect or creed or religion. It works the same for all of them. The law does not save anyone based on their religion or based on their prayers. Whatever the religion you belong to, you, your prayers definitely are meant to bring some discipline in your life, but do you get disciplined? It is your problem, if you are not disciplined. Then after crossing certain limits; definitely Nature would act to punish you in some form. You may not have the eye and perception to know that it is Nature who gave you the punishment, but you know deep within, that the punishment came to correct you.

Dharma is a Sanskrit word but does not mean it belongs to India and Hinduism or some religion. Dharma means it is LAW OF NATURE. It will act as per its algorithm and it will work for all equally without any partiality.

You cannot list down the actions of Dharma and if that is the way, millions of pages of books also, will fall short.

By taking the help of cosmic CEO, and the driver, Hari, you as Arjuna, can function as per Dharma well in your business and life that will get you prosperity.

Chapter-19

Change In Cosmic Management

Change in cosmic management does not mean that it is the change of person, like the way it happens in our companies.

The software of the CEO and the changes in his style of management would change as per time and space and its evolution of the world. As per change in its energy, style and approach of managing the cosmos, that specific energy is named something. That energy works in the background, spiritually. You cannot understand its work with normal eye and mind. You as CEO, your work cannot be seen by normal employees of your incorporation. They only get to see their immediate managers and leaders. But silently in the background, it is the CEO's plan and strategy that works throughout your company. In the same way, the work of the cosmic CEO cannot be perceived by normal human. It requires a spiritual eye to perceive and experience his work. God's work is also not perceived like that by all people.

Coming back to the thread of change in cosmic management and its style, currently the management is in the hands of "next incarnation of God or CEO" who is given the cosmic management to bring required harmony in the cosmos.

That next and last incarnation of God is Kalki. Kalki means, he is of time and no other earlier incarnation of his had such name. Time moves at speed and so is his software that works like a car with high voltage and high speed in the chaotic traffic but yet, no one gets hurt nor the car gets hurt. But yet, it meets the laws of Nature.

The management of his energy and style has started working in cosmos to evolve the human consciousness quite faster to the next time and space of the world. The evolution of souls have far fallen behind from its required pace. Souls have lost their strong energies because of which their lifespan is reduced, their minds and intellects are not able to perceive the world properly. People do not have energies to change themselves. You need to little understand about the cosmic structure to know as to why the change in management is needed. Actually the change in management is scheduled to come much later but it has come a bit in advance due to the cosmic urgency.

The cosmos has positive side and negative side of management teams that work in spiritual realms in the form of souls. They do not have bodies because, they do not have such karma to take bodies and live in the world. The world moves through four eras and the management of three ages are given the chance to positive management team while the last age (the current one called Kaliyuga) is given to the Negative management team.

The strategy of both negative and positive sides is to balance the cosmos in terms of both energies. Everyone in the world evolves from negative side to the positive side and goes beyond both of them.

Whenever the imbalance reaches its dangerous levels, in these energies of the world the CEO comes down to protect the world and show the way to the world.

Due to negative energies and its management they have taken the world and its consciousness far behind by injecting negativity into the humans. Kali is the name of the ruler of negative energies. This age is named of him and he is such negative that his energies slip into everyone in the form of various gross bad habits, primarily which pave the way for subtle bad habits. Kali also means, of time. He is also of time and he also has that high speed of negativity to destruct the humanity. He has high advanced software of virus and to deal with him, same degree of antivirus has to come which is of Kalki.

He injects negativity into humans through, habits such as liquor drinking, smoking, doing drugs, womanizing, gambling and gold related transactions. These are the gross doors through which the bad habits enter into your system primarily. Kali's energy comes through them and slips silently into your system. Once you get into any of those doors, slowly they will introduce you to their much deeper subtle habits such as jealousy, anger, hatred, anxiety, lust, greed and all these. These are all basically brothers of the main gross level bad habits.

Kali's strategy is so subtle and you cannot identify that he is slipping into your system. He comes in the form of a friend or anyone who will introduce you to any of those and rest all will slip into your system so deeply which you cannot fight with.

Just take the example of smoking, you cannot fight with it and quit that bad habit. I am sure a friend must have introduced you to smoking. You have very weak soul energies which are not enough to fight that habit.

In old days, young people used smoke or drink by going far away from their neighborhoods. But as the time changed, this generation has started doing all these in the house, in front of elders. Now those bad habits became so morally legalized, that parents and children together participate in doing them. Such morally legalized, those bad habits, in the society today. They cannot be fought so easily. If there is a good boy who does not have these bad habits, now he is considered to be bad and he is considered to be not grown up or considered as mismatch in the society. So out of hundred if you find one such man, he does not have any energy and he is changed to adopt those habits easily because of the social pressures. That's how, the whole society has spoiled now and that is directly having impact on the life span of man, his status of mind, way of living life and way of conducting his business and all.

Reduction of lifespan of man is a quite dangerous scenario for humanity and Nature. It's like crop of souls for the Nature. The yield of the Soul-Crop, would be quite less for the Nature whereas the number of crop cycles will increase for Nature. So humans and even all other species would have great impact in the number of births they take. The lifespan of man will fall down to even 30 years in future which is has a great impact on all lives on the earth and it is a great loss for the Nature especially. The whole evolution gets disturbed in Nature in which even several other living beings live.

So, that negative energy and its management wants to totally make all people go against the laws of Nature. If that is the case, the whole cosmic system cannot survive. The question of existence is coming to humanity. It is like imagine, your liver and lungs working against you and the laws of your body. Obviously you cannot survive for long, One day, the question of your existence comes as the bad operations of those both organs would totally fail and damage all the other organs as well and then, one day you will lose your life.

In your case if you are weak, obviously you cannot take action against such bad actions of your organs. But in case of Nature it is not like that. Nature has a huge history and carries mighty energies in her womb. Initially it tries to fix the problems through various small energies like bringing down some spiritual gurus and teaching the humanity to transform. When the time is lost and if Nature is not getting balanced, then it will call the owner of the cosmos, whom we call God.

When he comes down, he comes down and applies various approaches in his own styles. He would even have the capability of bringing new technologies for soul evolution. He may not even teach, but his just existence like SUN would transmit the energies to people that will transform their consciousness.

Especially of Kalki, his main technology is transforming the human consciousness involuntarily, as the whole Nature will start pushing the humanity, in his management directions.

Many people do meditation, you think, meditation is done? Do you really have the energy to practice meditation? Most of the people through various methods and techniques go to some level of meditation and they get some temporary peace and happiness for few minutes. But after coming out of such meditation, they again get into the world doing the same bad actions and deal with people, by going against the laws of Nature. Such actions of theirs would totally make them loose their peace that they earn in the meditation. It means, such meditational practices and efforts are no longer taking their evolution forward.

I am sure after your morning yoga and meditation, you go to office and you deal with various people and by midday you would lose your peace. You get back home in the night and when you start doing meditation; all your actions and people appear in your mind that does not let you get into deeper levels of meditation. Actually meditation needs to happen. Meditation is not done.

The change in new management given to Kalki, the god and the ruler of the cosmos now has started his work in the spiritual realm which you cannot perceive by your gross senses.

One of his works is to transform the human consciousness involuntarily. Since you do not have energies to meditate and you are not able to meditate now, it happens with you involuntarily with the help of cosmic energy, and then you can surely evolve. Imagine, meditation happening in you, as you watch TV naturally. Imagine meditation happening as you sleep and you are aware of it. Meditation is only, one of his works. There are several other things such as people whom you meet, the situations, your karma, your traits and all those matter. Imagine all of them are involuntarily operated to evolve your consciousness. Then obviously you will not deal with people, after going to office in a bad way or others do not interact with you that disturb your peace. There are several involuntary operations that he does as the cosmic CEO with his divine management team. Such operations evolve the human consciousness much faster.

His involuntary way of working is happening through "Hariom Movement" which you can check at www.hariom.life

The two mantras that are given to you in this book, is to bring that transformation in you, so you will be able to prosper. The involuntary evolution technology is brought down to bring faster evolution in the human consciousness that adds value in your material life.

Kalki the cosmic CEO has got his own strategies and style of working against the negative energy of Kali. Both Kalki and Kali sound nearer to each other. Both of them are connected with "kaal" which means time in Sanskrit. One is the positive king of the cosmos by the name Kalki and the other negative king to ruin the world with the name Kali.

The mantras that are given to you Hariom and "Hariom, Hare Kalki, Hare Rama, Hare Krishna, Hare Hare" will bring involuntary transformation in your life. All you have to do just chanting these two mantras by which you get tuned to his frequency and you would receive divine energies form his source that will transform you naturally and involuntarily.

Kalki's work as the new cosmic CEO has started in the spiritual realm that goes for several years which will clean the world to a greater extent and make the world ready so that he can descend later physically. So before his physical appearance, he is preparing grounds in the world, working mainly in the realm of consciousness.

Hariom is such missions of the God CEO, Naryana or Krishna or Hari. Hariom movement is not run by human effort. It is run and managed by the divine effort of Lord Hari, the CEO of the cosmos.

Tune to his frequency with the mantras, Hariom and "Hariom, Hare Kakli, Hare Rama, Hare Krishna Hare Hare ". You will find the transformation happening in your life automatically.

Chapter-20

Making The Nature Work For You

When you tune to the frequency of the cosmic CEO, you start adopting the personality of God, the Super CEO automatically by which you will effectively and efficiently take care of your incorporation being in attached-detached mode of personality.

As you keep chanting the two mantras given, you will find the change in your personality automatically. You will start finding new abilities being loaded into you. You will find extraordinary expertise and skills loaded into you automatically. You will find yourself more like following the laws of Nature automatically. You do not have to practice major spirituality. Some practices are given in the online transformation workshop of "Hari Om Movement", which will help you get the involuntary software of cosmic CEO, by which you will find more abilities loading in to you.

As you find transformation and discipline falling in your life automatically, you will find that Nature cooperating with you, your thoughts and decisions.

Devendra is the king of all divine energies. Sun is doing his universal job based on the energies and the cooperation he gets from the Nature. He gets unlimited energies from Nature. No one can fight with the Sun easily. So, imagine you becoming like that Sun who is doing his cosmic job. Whole Nature stands with you in accomplishing what you want.

Your thoughts, intentions and wishes for your company will automatically manifest in the real world, which happens with the cosmic energy being with you and cooperating with you all times. Imagine you are not just an ordinary CEO but a CEO loaded with divine energies and who has the support of the whole Nature. Then you become like Arjuna. All weapons would be at your call and for all your actions; there will be a cosmic background.

Nature is the actual force that is meant to connect all people to various situations as per their Karma. It is the main force behind every positive action taking place in the world.

Imagine such force being there with you all times. You can expect sales taking place automatically, more business deals happening automatically, expansion of business happening automatically and cooperation from your employees happening, automatically and so on. You will find people coming to you automatically, doing things that you want. You think of so and so activity being needed in your organization and you will find its manifestation taking place automatically with the help of various people. Some people will come forward to do those actions automatically. It is the force of Nature that works behind them.

Nature will work immensely behind all actions of the souls who want to do universal jobs. When you transform from a personal CEO to Arjuna, the whole Nature will work for you.

You can make people work for you but, you must have not heard anywhere about making forces of Nature working for you!

That will happen when you start transforming as Arjuna. While you are asleep, you will find your consciousness working with the help of the Nature and its seabed of universal consciousness. You may experience some dreams kind of visuals which are not actually dreams. They are actually some actions arranged by Nature in the world of consciousness. Those actions can only be perceived if you get into high end of Meditation which is Samadhi.

But you will experience them while you are asleep and you will feel them like dreams. You will find some fixes for your problems in the realm of integrated consciousness of the whole world like the movie inception. Do not think that you will have such abilities to do bad actions out of illusion. But the operation of it remains in the hands of your cosmic driver, Krishna. He knows best what is Dharma and what you and your corporation need. So accordingly he will do some inception job in the integrated consciousness. You can only enjoy its fruits but you can never get the operation of it, into your hands. In the realm of consciousness, you will find your soul meeting some people in your office and working with them in the background. As the days pass by, you will find some problems in your company resolved. It is actually the combination of your works in the real world and also the work of your soul in the spiritual world with the help of Nature and the cosmic CEO. Do not take this in negative way, as if you are doing some bad actions or actions against somebody's will like that movie, Inception. But the actions in your case would be for the benefit of your incorporation and the world with positive intentions, which is operated by the Nature and the cosmic CEO, but not by you.

You need to understand a little about intentions and actions. Actions may appear to be like negative. For example you may slap someone with the intention that his tooth ache should go away. But for the people who see that action and also for the one who received that action from you appears that you are negative. But you are positive and the action of yours would actually benefit the one who received that action from you. So you basically have hit the other person with good intention but the action may appear to be negative in the real world.

In the case of a bad man with bad intention also, the action will be same like yours. Imagine a bad man hitting someone with bad intention of hurting him. Then intention and action both are bad in his case.

World is used to see the second case but not the first case explained above. Some of the divine actions especially with incarnations would be similar to that of the first case, said above.

So, good intention, love behind the action and action for the benefit of the others, is very essential in your actions. Actions as such would greatly benefit the world.

So understand that your soul actions in the spiritual world with the help of Nature and the Cosmic CEO are only intended and meant for resolving problems in your corporation, in your personal life and also in the world. So, after reading about that inception job of Nature, in case you are carrying any bad impressions, you can remove them from your mind.

Also, these soul actions will only happen when your consciousness expands in the Nature and only when you carry positive intentions and positive thoughts.

After chanting the mantras given, if you have positive mind, universal mind and positive thoughts only then, Nature and the Cosmic CEO's energies will help you in both real world and in the spiritual world. If you carry negative thoughts even to a slight extent, your energies will start getting unloaded and you will also find that the cooperation of the Nature and the Cosmic CEO, moving away from you. So the cosmic CEO will NOT help you if you have bad intentions and bad thoughts about people in the world.

If you try to cheat others, trick others or suppress others or your colleagues, if you try to hurt others or if you want to favor only certain people etc. are considered by Nature as actions of your weak and possessive personality. Then, Nature will not work with you and help you in your actions. Cosmic CEO will only help you when your thoughts, intentions and actions are positive and are meant for the welfare of others.

After experiencing some changes and transformation in your life, by chanting the two mantras given, if you want to further pursue the next level technologies of taking the help of the cosmic CEO and Nature, you can probably take up online transformation courses which you can practice from home. The online workshop is offered by Hariom Movement. You can check the website www.hariom.life for more information.

Hariom

movement

Involuntary Transformation

www.hariom.life

www.ingramcontent.com/pod-product-compliance
Ingram Content Group UK Ltd.
Pitfield, Milton Keynes, MK11 3LW, UK
UKHW021650190726
13853UKWH00001B/167

9 789390 489602